T. C. Arthur

Reminiscences of an Indian Police Official

T. C. Arthur

Reminiscences of an Indian Police Official

ISBN/EAN: 9783337062019

Printed in Europe, USA, Canada, Australia, Japan

Cover: Foto ©ninafisch / pixelio.de

More available books at **www.hansebooks.com**

THE FORT OF VIZIADROOG.

Frontispiece.

REMINISCENCES

OF AN

INDIAN POLICE OFFICIAL

BY

T. C. ARTHUR

Illustrated

BY

HORACE VAN RUITH, Esq.

AND

E. M. CAUTLEY

LONDON
SAMPSON LOW, MARSTON & COMPANY
LIMITED
St. Dunstan's House
FETTER LANE, FLEET STREET, E.C.
1894

LONDON:
PRINTED BY WILLIAM CLOWES AND SONS, LIMITED, STAMFORD STREET
AND CHARING CROSS.

PREFACE.

It is to be regretted that old Anglo-Indian Officials, especially those whose lives have been passed in the interior as Magistrates, Superintendents of Police, and the like, do not more often employ the time, that we are told hangs so heavily on their hands after retirement, in jotting down some of their experiences for the benefit of the public in England, whose ideas of Official life in India, of the mode in which the country is governed, and of the idiosyncrasies of its people are still of the crudest.

Especially as to the "seamy side" of the character of the mixed population could police officers contribute much that would not only be very good reading, but that would also prove highly instructive to their younger brethren just commencing life.

General Hervey, who was for many years employed in the Department for the Suppression of Thuggee, has recently set an admirable example of what might be done in that direction.

It is true that incidents rarely occur in India which would furnish material for tales "à la Gaboriau," or that could vie in interest with the

"Hansom Cab Mystery." Highly scientific murder is happily as yet unknown in India; jewels worth fabulous amounts are not often made away with;* the trained intelligence of detective geniuses of the Lecocq type is rarely called for—which is fortunate, inasmuch as the Indian police, as at present organised, is destitute of the detective element, as understood in Europe.

A very rough-and-ready investigation ordinarily suffices to bring home his guilt to the average Indian criminal. As a matter of fact, the commoner offences—murders, manslaughters, and thefts—have usually been traced to the perpetrators before the constable makes his appearance, and he finds that the patel (or head man) and the humble mhár (village watchman) have already got the offender in custody. It only remains for the constable to get the case into order and to supply—which he is very ingenious in doing—any gaps in the chain of evidence. After this it runs the usual monotonous course—to the nearest Magistrate or to the Sessions, as the case may be.

But, as every experienced Official knows, there are thousands of serious crimes that are not only never discovered, but never even reported; there are many reported that never occurred; and careful observation over a number of years shows that there are flushes or epidemics, as it were, of particular classes of crime, and there are others which are peculiar to particular castes and races.

* Though His Royal Highness the Duke of Connaught was robbed of valuable jewels between Rawal-Pindi and Poona.

If a few leading cases from the note-book of an old Anglo-Indian Police Official in the Bombay Presidency can throw any light on any of these matters, I shall rejoice that my scribblings during a long period of sickness and suffering have not been entirely useless.

No one can live for thirty-five years in India without being drawn into deep sympathy with the people, without recognising the many virtues they possess, and the numerous good qualities which have survived ages of anarchy and persecution. It is in no hostile spirit, therefore, that allusion will hereafter be made to certain weaknesses, certain conspicuous failings of character, which force themselves to the front. They are largely compensated for by good traits; such as unbounded hospitality, kindliness of disposition, the rugged fidelity of the servant to his master, which come back to our minds in very practical form when we have left India for good. It is my earnest hope that in bringing out the darker side of Indian character I may also have thrown light on some of the better qualities of the people among whom I have lived so long.

On the other hand, I trust I may have shown the need for incessant watchfulness in the administration of a conglomeration of nationalities, creeds and castes such as exist in India. We habitually shut our eyes in India—as in other Colonies—believe that all is going on for the best, and abhor pessimists. But, trite saying though it be, that in India we walk on a slumbering volcano—the truth of it is now and again brought home to us with startling vividness, and an incident here or there reveals to us, for the moment, the glow of the molten mass on the crust of which we walk so blithely.

In these pages, I have endeavoured with all humility to utter certain warnings which, even a year ago, would have been denounced as mere ravings. Yet they have been justified very amply since! And on this very day when I despatch my last proof, an ominous cloud hangs over the dominions of Her Majesty the Queen Empress. It may—let us hope that it will—disperse.

T. C. ARTHUR.

11*th May*, 1894.

P.S.—The following tales are not "stories," or in any sense inventions. I could give chapter and verse, could refer to existing records in verification of them; and although it has been necessary to give fictitious names occasionally, I can assure my readers that in almost every case I was personally concerned, and that the others in some way or other came under my personal cognizance.

CONTENTS.

CHAPTER I.

VINDICTIVENESS.—ANONYMOUS LETTERS.—THE WOULD-BE PARRICIDE.

PAGE

Vindictiveness the chief cause of crime in India.—Anonymous letters main instrument.—The difficulty in dealing with them.—Two examples of conspiracies originating in such letters, and discovery of original conspiracy by means of the second.—The would-be parricide.—Madhowrao Khote.—His family troubles.—Description of Narrayengaum.—His son Vinayek Deo's disappearance.—Anonymous letter accusing his father of his murder.—Confessions of two accomplices.—Madhowrao arrested.—Disbelief of all officials in the confessions.—Chief Constable takes leave.—Constant remands.—Indignation of the Sudder Court.—Peremptory orders to commit for trial to sessions.—Chief Constable returns in nick of time with missing man.—His identification.—Grand climax.—Madhowrao discharged.—Vinayek Deo and two approvers committed for trial and sentenced . . 1

CHAPTER II.

THE GREAT MILITARY PENSION FRAUDS.

PART I.

Anonymous letter containing true information followed up for two years.—Discovery of an organized system of fraud of long standing.—South Konkan the recruiting ground of Bombay army.—Consequent location of Military Pension Paymasters' establishment in Dapoolie.—Colt becomes assistant collector.—He receives anonymous letter.—Is supposed to have followed usual course about pension matters.—He takes up his residence at Dapoolie next to Pension Paymaster's office.—Colt's *coup*.—Report to Government.—Military Court of Enquiry ordered . 16

CHAPTER III.

THE GREAT MILITARY PENSION FRAUDS.—*continued.*

PART II.

PAGE

Details of Colt's grand *coup*.—His remarkable secrecy and apparent neglect of the first anonymous letter.—The wisdom of it.—Colt's means of information.—Mr. Daniel Monk.—Fulloo Parsi.—Description of the system of paying pensioners.—The certificate of honour.—Ignoring it.—The result.—The Sowkars take advantage.—The office clerks fall in.—The Sowkars distrust pensioners.—Dummy system grows up.—Tannak the chief dummy.—All caught in the act.—The Court assembles.—Sealed orders found tampered with at first meeting.—Government order the suspension of the whole office, and the Court itself to pay pensions 25

CHAPTER IV.

THE GREAT MILITARY PENSION FRAUDS.—*continued.*

PART III.

The Court adjourns *sine die* to take over the paymaster's duties.—Colt meanwhile takes up the original anonymous letter.—Deceased pensioners' pension found to have been drawn for seven years after his death by village officers.—Colt commits them to sessions and returns to Dapoolie.—Court reassembles.—Colt leads off by putting in copies of proceedings in above case.—Ramnàk Bhàgnàk Subedar-major and Sirdar Bahadur.—Effect of his evidence.—Hundreds more witnesses.—Court proceeds to Chiploon.—Court makes its first report.—Copy sent to office establishment.—Absurd discomfiture of Major.—The Paymaster on being confronted with Tannak.—Delay of clerks in submitting their defence.—It is delivered at last, and Court closes to prepare report.—Colt obliged to go elsewhere on duty.—Accidentally meets a Soukar in bazaar evening before departure.—Secretly puts it off.—Fulloo Parsi gives important news of clerks intended action next morning.—Colt takes farewell of all.—Pretends to ride away, but returns by a circuitous route and conceals himself.—Clerks come to present petition.—Colt suddenly reappears.—Mysterious Soukar and the Cassee forgery incident.—Grand climax 41

CHAPTER V.

BUSSAPA'S REVENGE.

PAGE

Yellapa the cotton-farmer.—His son Bussapa.—The cotton mania and its extravagances.—Silver galore.—Trotting matches.—Red silk umbrellas.—Drink.—Yellapa dies.—Cotton down to nothing.—Bussapa in difficulties.—His little son Bhow.—Bussapa's chief creditor Dewchund's great attachment for Bhow.—Dewchund puts on the screw.—Violence of Bussapa.—He drinks excessively.—Dewchund threatens foreclosure in three days.—Diabolical idea of Bussapa.—Is put into force.—Bhow's murder.—Bussapa takes the body to Dewchund's shop.—His idea of payment in full.—Further devilish scheme of Bussapa.—Is carried out.—Dewchund accused of Bhow's murder.—Narrowly escapes.—Bussapa's end 52

CHAPTER VI.

UNDISCOVERED MURDER, UNPUNISHED MURDER, AND KIDNAPPING.

Undiscovered murder.—Hard nuts to crack.—Comparison of English and Indian undiscovered crime.—Not unfavourable to India on the whole.—Kidnapping of concubines.—Balloo's wife sold by Patel.—Balloo becomes uneasy at her absence.—Makes personal enquiries.—Patel knocks him on the head.—Conviction of Balloo frustrated by Native State.—Vigorous steps taken by Government and numerous concubines found.—The mysterious murder of an old Marwarri money-lender.—Not the faintest clue.—The house again entered.—Police completely baffled.—Murder, suicide or accident.—Woman found dead.—Europeans falsely accused.—Probable solution.—Causes of failure.—Lack of detective element in police 62

CHAPTER VII.

THE MISSING TIGER; OR, CAIN AND ABEL.

Three quarters of the murders in India not reported.—Otherwise India compares favourably.—Want of detective agency.—Native dislike of delays in procedure.—They used to combine to conceal crime.—Much improvement nowadays.—Justice much better administered on the whole in Bombay Presidency than in England.—Labouchere's magisterial pillory would lack material.—

Cain and Abel ; or, the missing tiger.—Meeting the "Ixpresh."
—Tiger killed one brother.—Carried off another.—Arrival at
village.—Plausible appearance of corpse of dead man.—All
hands to beat.—Caution in approaching spot where body was
found.—Accident to lawyer friend.—Tiger still missing.—Suspicion aroused.—Return to village and inquest by torchlight.
—Murder will out.—The mystery cleared up.—Cain caught.—
Missing tiger accounted for.—Cain shams mad.—Time goes on.
—Cain hanged.—Village plot 73

CHAPTER VIII.

THUGGEE.—THE MASSACRE.

Erroneous idea that Thuggee has not been stamped out, and that
poisoning has taken its place.—The coming famine.—Cattle
driven into the Nizam's territory for sale by six Mahrattas.—
Returning with cash they encounter an urbane Mahomedan
gentleman with servant who professes to be a police patrol.—
They accept his protection for two days.—The last supper.—
Discovery of one survivor.—Then of five other corpses.—All
poisoned by arsenic —Courteous Mahomedans never found . 83

CHAPTER IX.

CHILD-MURDER FOR ORNAMENTS.

Child murder for ornaments still common.—Indian "Mrs. Browns."
—Murderers usually Marwarrees and other lower trading castes.
—One Mahomedan case recalled to mind.—Poor little Saloo.—
His father's great friend murders him for the sake of a few
trinkets.—The accusing hand.—Suliman's remorse.—Hideous
case of kleptomania.—Reconciliation between Saloo's father and
Suliman.—Suliman's fate 89

CHAPTER X.

MURDER FROM JEALOUSY.—MURDER FROM INFIDELITY.

Murders from jealousy quite as common in England as in India.—
Rural morality better in India.—Common jealousy murder easily
detected.—Quilp.—His brutality to Bhagi.—Crowning brutality.
—Threat to cut off her nose next day.—Bhagi arranges with
her paramour.—Next evening Quilp is done to death and his
body is thrust into a lime kiln 94

CHAPTER XI.

FORGERY AND PERJURY.

PAGE

Forgery and its helpmeet perjury.—Ordinary perjury.—"Tutoring" common in India.—Comparative perjury in England and India.—Why not give the Indian a fair chance?—India is the land of forgers.—Some reasons for this being so.—Notable gang.—The eighteen.—Their detection.—The victims retaliate.—Discovery of a noted forger's stock-in-trade 99

CHAPTER XII.

DACOITY.

Dacoity in old days.—The Dusserah meeting.—Programme arranged.—Gradual suppression till mutiny broke out.—Recrudescence of Dacoity but under changed organisation.—Special officers.—The Bheel outbreak.—Bhagoji Naique.—Yesoo Bheel.—He attempts to restrain Bhagoji but in vain.—Becomes a Government informer.—The Amnesty.—Hanmant Bheel.—His virulence against Yesoo.—The plot of revenge.—Dreadful massacre . . 109

CHAPTER XIII.

WRECKING.

Piracy and wrecking, old style.—Sea Dacoity in England.—In India.—Plundering the wrecked.—Wrecking for insurance.—The Talekeri wreck.—First concealed.—Then disclosed by native Press.—Police first baffled.—A clue.—A novel procedure.—Prosecution of whole village.—Witnesses found.—Conviction.—Full restitution from village 121

CHAPTER XIV.

HOUSEBREAKING.

Housebreaking.—Heredity.—Remarkable case of Jánoo Naik.—The premises.—Patience of Jánoo.—The watchman Sewram does not believe in him.—Sewram hears a noise under the house one night.—Wakes his master at right moment.—Goes round to Jánoo's hut.—Finds the mined gallery and catches Jánoo just emerging from the hole.—His sons just inside.—There's many a slip between cup and lip 135

CHAPTER XV.

RIOTS.

Contrast between foreign travellers and the average British globe-trotter and their objects and opinions.—The ordinary Mahomedan and Hindu riot.—Causes of them.—Story of the riot at Dajipur.—Blank cartridge.—The absurdity of using it.—The uselessness of it at Dajipur.—D—— fires into the "brown of them" and orders ball cartridge.—Instant end of the riot.—The wounded man.—The trial.—The death of Mr. Prescott.—Danger of allowing any great assemblages.—Great need for constant watchfulness . 145

CHAPTER XVI.

FOREST ROBBERIES.

Dawn of forest conservancy.—Things went very well in those days.—The mutiny dislocates everything.—Enormous mischief since the fall of the Peishwa.—Unchecked up to 1863.—Ghattis.—Their system.—False ideas prevalent among the people.—Remarkable detection of extensive forest frauds by Inspector Bucket.—The contract felling system.—Easily utilised for fraud.—Inspector Bucket reveals the plot.—Timber and firewood of great value found secreted in the forests.—Ballaji and Co. secrete their real books.—The session's trial.—The Judge acquits.—Government appeal against acquittal.—Successful result.—Inspector Bucket subsequently finds the missing real books, and prosecutes successfully 159

CHAPTER XVII.

THE PREDATORY TRIBES.

The Government find time in the early "fifties" to attend to crime.—General Hervey.—His labours.—His success.—His books.—Petty maurauders break up.—Migratory and non-migratory.—System pursued by the former.—Specimen of their habits.—Villagers at last show fight.—A goodly list of loot.—Non-migratory.—Attempts to reclaim them by Native Governments.—Bamptias.—Oochlias and the like.—Tricks upon travellers.—I am myself victimised.—The feint by night surprise.—"Tim" bones the intruder.—But accomplices meantime clear out my tent.—Humbled exceedingly.—New field daily extending for the ability of these rogues 172

CHAPTER XVIII.

CRIME DURING THE FAMINE.

PAGE

Retrospect of the Deccan famine.—Revival of Dacoity at the outset with signs of organisation as of old.—Safety of the bullion consignments by mail carts.—Tribute to the courage of the Parsi contractors, and to their generosity.—When relief operations were in full working order, Dacoity rapidly declined, except near Great Indian Peninsular Railway Lines.—Beginning of looting grain trains on heavy inclines.—Gradual demoralisation of subordinate railway staff.—False consignments.—Heavy losses to Great Indian Peninsular Railway Company.—Government Railway Commission.—Its report.—Company can now never be similarly exploited 185

CHAPTER XIX.

DISARMING.

The disarming of the people.—Why no disarmament had ever before been attempted.—Motives of policy.—Gradual discontinuance of the practice of arms.—Nevertheless arms highly prized.—Agriculturists very loath to register heirlooms.—Preferring to have them broken up and returned in prizes.—Pathetic scenes.—Great difficulty in disarming towns known to be full of arms where little registration had taken place.—Sangamnair notorious.—A Madras military pensioner gives good information.—Great finds.—Findings in the streets next morning 195

CHAPTER XX.

AGRARIAN CRIME.

Agrarian crime in the Irish sense little known.—Boycotting for Agrarian reasons also unknown.—No knowing, however, what National Congress may effect.—Courts of Justice the present arena.—But occasional outrages occur.—Women and children, however, never molested in India.—Startling discovery in a condemned cell.—The condemned's last will and testament.—The history of Vithal Prahbu Desai 205

CHAPTER XXI.

JAILS.

Indian jails much improved of late.—Old system of sending long term convicts to Bombay from the Straits Settlements.—A model jailor.—His peculiar mode of discipline so successful.—Two convicts, a Chinaman and a Malay have a deadly feud.—The Malay lies in wait.—Runs " Amok."—Is ingeniously caught alive.—The convict Joker.—Singular virtues of the "Cat" . 214

CHAPTER XXII.

LOAFERS.

Part I.

Crows with guinea-fowl eggs.—Police and village head men with loafers.—Arrival of harmless loafer in village.—Conversation.—Profuse hospitality of Patel.—Loafer sleeps the sleep of the just.—Policeman arrives on the scene.—Does not get much change out of loafer.—Will report to the Burra Saheb.—Loafer laughs him to scorn.—Toothsome supper again supplied by village.—Loafer flits and continues his objectless journey to nowhere in particular.—Short career of violent loafer.—Death of one of them.—His last words.—The mysterious loafer.—Eludes our vigilance.—Appeal to Blank Johnson, Esqre. . . 227

CHAPTER XXIII.

LOAFERS.

Part II.

Loafers in recent years.—The share mania.—How it attracted loafers to the city of Bombay.—They become a public nuisance.—Are legislated for.—Amusing case.—A loafer accuses himself falsely of robbing a Government treasury during the mutiny.—Collins.—Remarkable illustration of the generosity of natives to poor whites during the Prince of Wales' visit.—Proof that they are also grateful 242

CHAPTER XXIV.

RECEIVERS OF STOLEN GOODS AND COINERS.

PAGE

The Fagin class of receivers not existent in India but ordinary "fences" innumerable.—The nearest approach to Fagin in Military Cantonments.—His connection with Tommy Atkins.—Personal experience of this connection.—The "puir laddie's" holiday spoiled.—Coiners.—General Hervey on coining.—Great improvement in appearance of false coin and false notes since the General wrote.—Probability of forging currency notes increasing. —My own experience 252

CHAPTER XXV.

MISCELLANEOUS.

The fighting qualities of the police.—Gallantry when led by European officers.—The multifarious duties of the police.—Collecting Spanish fly.—Curing snake bites and killing them.—The Foorsa. —The Cobra.—The chain viper.—Police services in the famine notorious.—The locust plague.—The rat plague.—Only some of the extra duties which are cheerfully performed . . . 260

CHAPTER XXVI.

CONCLUSION.

Résumé of necessary reforms.—Young gentlemen from England not wanted.—Why should these things be?—Reply.—The cogwheel system.—Very good for India.—Lord Lansdowne's portentous farewell words.—It is understood that Police Reform is now engrossing the attention of several Governments, including that of Bombay.—The cloud before the storm and how to disperse it . 276

LIST OF ILLUSTRATIONS.

FULL-PAGE ILLUSTRATIONS.

		To face page
THE FORT OF VIZIADROOG	E. M. Cautley	Frontispiece
NARRAYEN-GAUM	,,	6
THE IDENTIFICATION IN THE FORT	H. Van Ruith	12
DAPOOLIE: PAYING THE PENSIONERS	E. M. Cautley	29
LES NOUVEAUX RICHES	H. Van Ruith	53
BUSSAPA'S REVENGE	,,	59
THE FATAL DELL	E. M. Cautley	64
SEVERNDROOG, ALSO KNOWN AS HURNEE, FROM THE TOMB OF TULAJI ANGRIA	E. M. Cautley	68
THE INQUEST: "MURDER WILL OUT"	H. Van Ruith	80
THE LAST SUPPER	E. M. Cautley	86
THE DENOUNCING HAND	,,	91
THE BHEEL'S REVENGE	,,	120
ANGRIA'S COLÁBÁ	,,	126
THE WRECK AT TALEKERI	,,	128
CAUGHT AT WORK	H. Van Ruith	141
THE RIOT	,,	151
SECRET FOREST HOARDS	E. M. Cautley	166
THE NIGHT'S SURPRISE: "TIM'S GOT HIM!"	,,	182
ROBBERY OF OVERLADEN GRAIN TRAINS DURING THE FAMINE	H. Van Ruith	190
DISARMING	,,	198
CATCHING HIM ALIVE	,,	221
LOAFER MAKES HIMSELF AT HOME	,,	230
THE MYSTERIOUS STRANGER	,,	237
JINJIRA (HABSÁN)	,,	240

ILLUSTRATIONS IN TEXT.

		PAGE
TANNAK	E. M. Cautley	34
BHOW AT DEWCHUND'S SHOP	H. Van Ruith	55
MEETING THE "IXPRESH"	,,	77
SULIMAN'S FATE	E. M. Cautley	93
THE FORGER'S STOCK-IN-TRADE	H. Van Ruith	107
YESOO BHEEL	E. M. Cautley	116
SEWRAM HEARS SOMETHING	H. Van Ruith	140
INSPECTOR "BUCKET"	,,	167
"TIM" ON DUTY	E. M. Cautley	172
NOCTURNAL DEPOSITS		204
THE MODEL JAILOR	H. Van Ruith	216
PUZZLED CROWS	,,	228
"THEY WOS VERY GOOD TO ME, THEY WOS"	,,	234
COLLINS	From a Photograph	248
COBRA ON STRIKE	H. Van Ruith	264
DABOIA ELEGANS, OR CHAIN VIPER	,,	265
THE LOCUST	,,	268
GERBILLE INDICA, OR JERBOA RAT	,,	272
"SAHEB! BURRA DIBBIL ÁTÁ"	,,	284

REMINISCENCES

OF AN

INDIAN POLICE OFFICIAL.

CHAPTER I.

VINDICTIVENESS.—ANONYMOUS LETTERS.—THE
WOULD-BE PARRICIDE.

Anonymous Letters.

LOOKING back on all these years, I have come to the conclusion that by far the worst feature in native character is vindictiveness, and that it accounts for nearly all the worst crimes in the calendar. The slightest thing arouses it, and it stops at nothing. Its favourite arena is the criminal court, its favourite weapon anonymous accusation.

I wonder how many anonymous letters are received in the public offices in India in a single day, and how many of them have the smallest foundation of fact!

Yet it is by no means safe, especially for a Police Officer, to disregard this means of obtaining information; but it requires no little judgment and discrimination in dealing with it. At least ninety out of a hundred are vague, scurrilous, obviously malicious, and untrue, and can be at once consigned to the waste-paper basket. A small percentage may serve as warnings, or to put an Officer on his guard against events that are about to happen, or to indicate public feeling in disturbed times; a very small number will relate facts, or will make specific accusations supported by evidence that can be verified.

These last must, of course, be inquired into promptly, but with the utmost caution, lest grievous wrong be done to innocent persons. In most such cases it will sooner or later be discovered that the "bin name urzi," or anonymous letter, was the first step in an elaborate and diabolical conspiracy to injure an enemy.

I remember, for example, once receiving an anonymous letter accusing the "patel," or headman of a village, of having drowned a widow of his family, whose heir he was. Some dozen persons were named, some of whom were alleged to have witnessed the murder, others to have seen the patel throw the body into a disused well with a stone tied round its neck.

In the preliminary inquiry by a chief constable every one of the persons named gave evidence in accordance with the anonymous letter. But, to my mind, the evidence appeared far too good; and, hastening to the spot, I soon found that *none* of it could be true, and that the old widow had actually died of cholera, and had been cremated in the usual public manner.

Another anonymous letter received in the village informed me that the "kulkarnee," or village accountant, had got up the plot and drafted the first letter; his house was searched, and the rough draft in his handwriting was actually found among his papers. Ten of the gang were then indicted for conspiracy, and received heavy sentences at the sessions.

It is not often, however, that discovery is so rapid, and then grievous and prolonged suffering is unavoidably occasioned to the innocent accused. The following case, the record of which no doubt still exists in a certain sessions court, is so remarkable in every way that I shall relate it in detail, styling it—

The Would-be Parricide.

One beautiful evening in November I found myself at the end of a wearisome march under the Syadri Ghauts, or mountains, in the South Konkan. I had recently attained to the dignity of Acting Superintendent of Police, and, as a part of my duty, I had to travel over the spurs running down from the Ghauts, and to place here and there, at the most advantageous spots, as many police posts as the then new parsimonious police re-organisation scheme would admit.

The assistant collector was encamped in the village below, and I was to remain a few days with him to combine business with snipe shooting. Mr. Platt (as I shall call him) had been three or four years in charge of these same districts. Officials were not pitchforked about the Presidency in those good old days as they are now. An Assistant Collector and Magistrate had time thoroughly to know the people and to be known by them; whereas nowadays it is "*aj álé, oodya gélé, àsa chálalé*" (come to-day, gone to-morrow, so it goes on).

Mr. Platt had often spoken to me of the village of Narrayengaum as an exceptionally good camp, and of Madhowrao, the "Khote," or middleman, as the best specimen of the old-fashioned Brahmin he had ever met. Madhowrao paid us a long visit after dinner, and I found him all that Platt had described—a kindly, courtly native gentleman, of about sixty years of age, above the average height, of spare but still active frame, with the intellectual, well-cut features and the curious green-grey eyes peculiar to the Chitpawan Brahmin.

Platt had previously told me the history of the family, which had received this village in "Khoti" tenure about a century before as a reward for great services to the then Peshwa, and had settled down there to reclaim and repopulate it as stipulated in the "Sanad," or deed of grant. Madhowrao's elder and only brother had died a few months before. It had been the boast of the two brothers that no process of the revenue, civil or criminal courts, had ever been sent to Narrayengaum, and that no policeman ever visited it on duty.

But the burden of Madhowrao's lament to us that

night was that all this had changed for the worse since his brother's death. His brother left a son, then about twenty-five years of age, whom we saw, and set down then and there as a most objectionable specimen of the youthful Brahmin of the new school. Madhowrao also had a son of about the same age, whom we did not see. His father was in great trouble about him; he told us that Vinayek had for eight or ten years caused him the greatest anxiety by absenting himself for months together, and wandering about the country as a sort of "Gosai," or religious mendicant; he would suddenly return, and as suddenly disappear.

He had in this way disappeared after a two months' visit in the previous month of July, and Madhowrao was getting very anxious about him. We learnt that since his uncle's death, Vinayek, now known as Vinayek Deo (Deo is a religious affix), had become very intimate with his cousin, and that the two had combined to put pressure on him to consent to a partition or "Wantup" of the village. In short, poor Madhowrao seemed to me to be worried out of his life by his son and nephew. I may mention that—his wife having died some years before—his household was superintended by his widowed sister, a nice-looking old lady, who insisted on our eating some very pungent cakes of her own making. I remember that she bored us a good deal with her reiterated abuse of the missing Vinayek Deo, and it was clear that they were on the worst possible terms.

I must here, for the sake of my story, describe the locality, and I should be tempted, if space permitted, to dwell at some length on the great natural beauties of the spot. The village lay at the head of a gorge or ravine, just below where a stream, of considerable volume even at that season, and a roaring, foaming torrent in the rains, tumbled over a precipice, about two hundred feet high, into a basin it had worn out below—a pool which, like all pools at the foot of waterfalls along the Ghauts, was popularly supposed to be of unfathomable depth, and to be the haunt of a monster alligator. On a rocky ledge near the top of the fall, and almost projecting over it, rose the fantastic outline of the laterite-built village temple, which, with its red-brown walls here and there covered with patches of delicate ferns, stood out in strong relief against the falling water and the brilliant verdure of the hillside. The village nestled under the hill on the left, nearly hidden from view by a dense thicket of bamboos, cocoa-nut trees, and rich, glossy-leaved mangoes. Two houses only stood on the right hand of the stream, that of Madhowrao, nearest the torrent; that of his nephew a hundred yards lower down, each surrounded by groves of the "areca," or betel-nut palm—"the straightest thing in nature," some one has called it, and certainly one of the most graceful of all our Indian palms. In the fair season it was an easy matter to cross the torrent-bed from stone to stone. In the monsoon, or rainy season, the only means of getting from the village to the Khote's houses was by a sort of suspension

NARRAYEN-GAUM. [To face p. 6.

bridge of bamboos. At that season, of course, the roar of the waterfall drowned every other noise in the village. Below the village the gorge spread out on either side into a sheet of rice fields, while the hillsides were terraced out with infinite labour into narrow plots for the growth of coarser grains. A fairer scene, a more picturesque spot, it is impossible to conceive. I left it with regret, little thinking that I should have to visit it again in a few months to inquire into the horrible murder of Vinayek Deo, alleged to have been committed by our respected old friends, his father Madhowrao and his old aunt.

For some time I heard nothing from or about the village. At last the chief constable, or "Foujdar," as he was termed in those days, reported that Madhowrao, having failed to trace his son, had applied to him for aid, and offered a small reward for intelligence of him. A notice, with a description of Vinayek Deo, was accordingly sent to neighbouring districts, and circulated throughout my own charge, but with no result.

Some months passed by, and I was at the headquarters station for the monsoon with all the other district officers, when it was reported by the same Foujdar that he had received by post an anonymous letter declaring, in the most circumstantial manner, that Vinayek Deo had been strangled in the dead of the night by his old father and aunt, and that, unable to dispose of or carry the body themselves, they had employed their two farm-servants, Baloo and Bapoo, to carry it to the torrent and cast it into the deep pool, where it would doubtless be discovered, if the " mugger " (alligator) had not eaten it!

The Foujdar went on to say that he had at once proceeded to the village, had interrogated Baloo and Bapoo, who confessed to having been called up by Madhowra, in the middle of a tempestuous night in the previous July, that they were shown Vinayek Deo lying dead, with protruding tongue and eyes, and a cord round his neck, that Madhowrao and the old woman besought them to throw the corpse into the pool close by, and that after stripping off the clothes, which Madhowrao rolled up and gave to the old woman—his sister—they tied a heavy stone round it and hurled the body into the water.

On this the Foujdar had, of course, apprehended Madhowrao, his sister, and the two servants, had the house searched, and found a bundle of clothing and a pair of sandals hidden away, and was engaged in dragging the pool as well as he could. "The Sahib might rely upon his energy and intelligence, but it would be a great satisfaction if the Sahib could come down himself."

Of course the Sahib went down, and never shall I forget what an awful journey I had! It was raining from twelve to eighteen inches a day; every small watercourse was a raging torrent, and the path in the lower lands, leading along narrow rice bunds, afforded scarcely any footing for my unhappy " tat " (pony). However, everything has an end, and after two long weary days' marching I reached Narrayengaum, and put up in the only shelter there was—an outhouse at Madhowrao's farm.

The Foujdar then produced a bundle full of bones he had just fished up from the pool, which we sealed up and sent off for examination by the Civil Surgeon, and then the prisoners were brought before me. I was shocked beyond measure at the utter collapse of Madhowrao. He only moaned, and seemed hardly able to articulate, and his old sister kept going from one fit of hysterics into another. Having had the statements of Baloo and Bapoo previously read to me by the Foujdar, I had each of these gentlemen brought into me separately, and his handcuffs removed. Then, ordering the police to stay outside, I made each of them tell his own tale in his own way, and each of them repeated in substance what I have above related. I found it impossible to shake them in any way—" they had seen their old master in sore trouble; he had asked them to help in getting rid of the body, and they naturally obeyed him; they knew nothing more; they had never told any one what had happened, and could not understand how it became known; they hoped the Sirkar would be merciful, and pardon them for telling the truth," and so on. The men were ordinary Kunbis (cultivators), of average intelligence, but they seemed to me rather to overdo their feelings of gratitude and devotion to Madhowrao. They repeated over and over the same story in nearly the same words. Their evidence, in a word, was too good, and I made up my mind at once that they were lying.

Duty, however, required me to take the case back with me to the Assistant, my old friend Platt. He too questioned the would-be approvers, failed to shake their evidence, and took them to the Magistrate, one of the most experienced officials then in India. Here again they related their story without deviating a hair's breadth. Yet the Magistrate and Platt were as convinced as I was that they were repeating a well-taught lesson!

At the Magistrate's desire, but very much against my own inclination, I transferred the Foujdar, and the police who had been with him at the inquiry, to other posts. The Magistrate took fresh steps to trace Vinayek Deo in the surrounding districts, while the prisoners were remanded from time to time for further investigation.

In due course the Civil Surgeon deposed that the bones found were those of a bullock, and it further transpired that the bundle of clothes (which undoubtedly had belonged to Vinayek Deo) were not found in any way concealed in Madhowrao's house—they were simply laid in his own chest with his own clothes. We had many interviews with Madhowrao, who now constantly repeated, " Jiwant hai, pun mee mèlya-shiwai nahi yènar " (He is alive, but he won't come till I am dead). A month or two passed, when the transferred Foujdar applied for three months' leave on medical certificate, his health having completely broken down (as he alleged) in consequence of his disgrace. With the Magistrate's consent I let him go, and I understood he had gone to a relative in Bombay.

The case by this time was practically out of my hands, and was borne on the monthly register of cases pending before Mr. Platt. These were the days of the old "Sudder Adawlut," now the High Court of Judicature, which was then famed for penning most offensive precepts and comments on the work of the Judges and Magistrates. This intelligent body soon noticed Mr. Platt's delay in disposing of the Narrayengaum murder case, and called for and received explanations which only made them more angry. Detailed reports were then called for, and the Magistrate was told that the Court were of opinion that, notwithstanding there was no *corpus delicti*, there was still ample evidence for the committal of the prisoners. A fierce paper war with the District Magistrate then ensued, and so time slipped on till November, when Platt was again on tour, leaving the four accused in the lock-up at headquarters. At last the Magistrate forwarded to him a peremptory order from the Sudder Court that he should forthwith commit the Narrayengaum murder case to the sessions, and report within fifteen days that he had done so.

What followed is best told in the following characteristic epistle, which I shortly after received from Platt:—

"You will be pining to hear from me the full details of the Narrayengaum murder case. I only wish you had been with me at the end, and could have seen how heavily I scored against those judicial fossils in Bombay.

"Well, when I received their idiotic and, as I think, illegal order to commit, I ordered Madhowrao and Co. to be sent down to Viziadroog to meet me on Monday the 1st inst. On the previous evening I was pitched at Pimpulgaum, that little village on the opposite side of the creek—you know the place, close to the track that comes down from Rajapoor beyond—when a couple of policemen with a prisoner arrived, and the naik (corporal) in a great state of excitement handed me a packet with "Zaroor-zaroor" (urgent, urgent) written all over it. It was from your old Foujdar on leave, telling me that he sent the missing Vinayek Deo, whom he had followed up and caught far away in the Nizam's territory! I never felt more like licking a man in my life than when I saw the venomous young reptile and remembered all poor Madhowrao had suffered.

"To cut a long story short, I took him over to Viziadroog in my boat next morning, warning the police not to say who he was, and immediately on arrival had up the four prisoners—Madhowrao, his sister, and the two approvers. You can picture the scene to yourself. The Court was held as usual under that big banian tree in the fort, and I began by telling Madhowrao that I had now received final orders to commit the case to the sessions, but that I myself was firmly convinced of his innocence, and believed that Vinayek Deo was alive, and would sooner or later turn up.

"You will understand that this little harangue was by way of preparing Madhowrao. He, poor fellow, only said, as he always had, 'He *is* alive, but he has killed me.' The old lady squatted speechless, with her saree (dress) covering her face, and those two hounds, Baloo and Bapoo, retained their usual brutally stolid demeanour. I beckoned to the police behind the prisoners, and Vinayek Deo was brought almost noiselessly up, when I said to Madhowrao, 'God is great! Look behind you, Baba!' He turned, saw his son, and fell flat on his face insensible. The old lady went off into screeching hysterics, but the two others, so far as I noticed, never moved a muscle of their countenances. We had the greatest difficulty in reviving poor old Madhowrao; in fact, I at one time feared he was a dead man. He was better, however, in the afternoon, though terribly weak, and I was able to resume proceedings with Vinayek Deo as prisoner No. 1, Baloo No. 2, and Bapo No. 3.

"Vinayek Deo made a clean breast of it, confessing that he and that evil-visaged cousin whom we saw at Narrayengaum last

THE IDENTIFICATION IN THE FORT. [*To face p.* 12.

year concocted the plot between them. Vinayek Deo was to disappear suddenly, and make his way in disguise to the Moglai (Nizam's dominion), and after a sufficient interval the cousin Luxmanrao was to get an anonymous petition sent in denouncing Madhowrao and the old lady. Baloo and Baboo were carefully coached up as to their story, and told not to vary it by a word, and were promised some land rent free when Madhowrao was disposed of. A more fiendish conspiracy never entered a Brahmin's brain! You will have heard that I had the cousin arrested, and I have just committed the lot to the sessions on a charge of conspiracy, but I fear the cousin Luxmanrao will get off, for there is nothing but the confessions of the other three against him.

"The Magistrate writes me that on his return to the Sudder's precept he gave them a lecture, which they will hardly venture to publish in their monthly proceedings. He adds that he was sorry he could not send on my report, as I asked him to do; it was really 'too cheeky'! You must 'keep very kind' on your Foujdar. God knows what would have been the end but for his pluck and intelligence!"

The end of the case was that Vinayek Deo was sentenced to seven years' and Baloo and Bapoo to three years' each hard labour, while the cousin was acquitted. Madhowrao and the old lady quite got over it, and lived for some years afterwards. The cousin, however, went on a pilgrimage to Benares and died there, so Madhowrao had peace for the last few years of his life. I did "keep kindness" on the Foujdar. He was rapidly promoted, and died in harness as a police inspector. He always declared that when he went on leave he had no clue whatever, but he was deeply impressed by Madhowrao's demeanour, and very angry at having been disgraced, and was determined to find Vinayek Deo if he was alive, or never return to service again. He first picked up a thread of intelligence at that sink of iniquity, Pandharpur, and his subsequent adventures in pursuit of the missing man would make a capital story in themselves.

In the present day, with improved means of communication by telegraph and otherwise, Vinayek Deo would probably have been found in a few weeks, and the plot would not have matured. Even if it had, under the existing Codes of Procedure, Madhowrao's suspense would not have been prolonged; the Magistrate would doubtless have committed the case for trial, but at the sessions the Judge would have certainly relied greatly upon the assessors' appreciation of the evidence of the two approvers and the surrounding circumstances, and Madhowrao would certainly have been acquitted, though he would have remained under a cloud till his rascally son turned up.

I was at great pains to satisfy myself whether Vinayek Deo's object really was to get his father convicted of his own murder. I hoped that his vindictiveness only went as far as seeking to involve his father in disgrace and suffering; but subsequent interviews with Vinayek Deo in gaol left me no room for doubt. The man himself was actually rather proud of his performance, and evidently enjoyed relating how the plot was hatched and carried out. He seemed to me positively to exult in all his father had suffered, and only to regret that his cousin had not shared his own fate.

As to the motives of the two servants, Baloo and Bapoo, I could never discover that they had any beyond those above-stated ; they were common labourers, possessed of no land of their own, and they firmly believed that Vinayek Deo and his cousin would reward them if they stuck to their story. They admitted that they bore no ill-will towards Madhowrao, in whose house they had lived for years, and who, as well as his old sister, had always treated them well. They were very little higher than animals as to intelligence, but had not the gratitude that animals show to those who feed them.

CHAPTER II.

THE GREAT MILITARY PENSION FRAUDS.— TANNAK : THE DUMMY PENSIONER.

Part I.

In the true history of "The Would-be Parricide" I sketched the progress of a conspiracy, the first step in which was an anonymous petition of the false and more common type. I now follow it up by an account of another, but a true anonymous letter, which in a great measure led to the disclosure of an organised system of fraud extending over many years.

It is necessary for the purposes of my narrative that I should accurately describe the localities. I might, without risk of injuring the feelings of any one, even give the real names of the actors in the drama, for nearly thirty-five years have passed away, and, with one exception, every one concerned has long left India and been gathered to his fathers; the record, however, no doubt remains preserved in the archives of the Military Department.

My own knowledge of the case is derived from the perusal of a copy of the proceedings of a Military Court of Inquiry at the time, and from notes furnished to me since by the chief person connected with the affair, whose permission I have obtained to make use of them. During the early stages I was, as the Police Officer of the district, necessarily cognisant of what was going on, but I had nothing officially to do with the inquiry, beyond furnishing a couple of the most intelligent and reliable of my constables to aid the Assistant Magistrate—men who, I am glad to remember, thoroughly justified my selection, and ultimately rose to posts of (to them) considerable emolument in the Bombay City Police.

In the days I speak of, the South Konkan, which properly includes the two "zillahs," or districts, of Kolaba and Rutnagherry, was the favourite recruiting-ground of the Bombay Army. The ranks were then filled with sturdy Mahrattas, descendants of Sivaji's invincible "Hedkaris," inhabiting the spurs and valleys below the great Syhadri range of mountains. Every regiment also contained many outcast mhars from the same region, excellent soldiers, many of whom rose to high rank.

All this, I am told, has now been changed; recruiting parties, though still sent into the district, find great difficulty in enlisting even the small proportion of undersized men that fastidious commissioned officers will now admit into their battalions. Eighty-two Bombay cotton mills and other factories and the railways have absorbed all the spare labour the Konkan can provide, and mhars and low castes fill the scavenger corps of the Bombay Health Department. Still, there must be thousands of military pensioners spread over this country, whose well-being should be the care of a humane Government; and if anything that appears in this paper draws the attention of authority to their condition, it will not have been penned in vain.

Nearly in the centre of this South Konkan, six miles from the sea-board and the little fair-season port of Hurnee, is the old cantonment of Dapoolie, formerly the chief of many small military posts dotted along the coast after our subjugation of the country between 1817 and 1819. Dapoolie survived them all, being selected, by reason of its position, as the headquarters of the Native Veteran Battalion, to which were drafted all invalided sepoys still capable of some light duty, but not yet entitled to full pension.

Dapoolie thus naturally became the headquarters also of the Pension Pay Department—a department of considerable importance even now, seeing that it pays away some six lakhs per annum, and in the days of which I speak swallowed up nearly the whole land revenue of the Rutnaghiri Zillah. The Paymaster, provided with a strong establishment of Purbhus, or clerks, resided here, and twice during the fair season was expected to visit the principal towns accessible from the sea-board, and at each of them to pay the pensioners in the neighbourhood, previously summoned for the purpose. At Dapoolie itself he made quarterly payments, and the majority of the pensioners were settled within fairly easy reach of the cantonment. The system had been in force for nearly twenty years, during most of which time the same officer had held the post of paymaster.

Instances of personating deceased pensioners had occasionally but rarely cropped up, and on the whole the military authorities had no reason to doubt that all was going well. Towards the end of the "fifties," the Native Veteran Battalion, or the "Guttram Phaltan," as natives called it, was abolished, having, I may mention, done very useful service during the Mutiny years, 1857 to 1859, when even the decrepit military pensioners joined them in taking all the Treasury and other stationary guards throughout the Konkan.

The abolition of the cantonment had been determined upon, and specific orders were expected every month. In the interim the Bazaar-master (an old European Officer of the battalion) remained in charge of the cantonment.

It was at this time that my friend, whom I shall call Colt, joined the district as Assistant Collector and Magistrate in charge of the northern "talookas," or sub-districts, wherein Dapoolie is situate. Colt was an officer of some few years' standing, endowed with remarkable energy; and though in no sense of the word a good Mahratti or Guzerati scholar, yet possessed of an unusual practical knowledge of both those vernaculars, especially of Mahratti, which he wrote and read easily, and spoke like a native. He was thus quite independent of his sheristedar (secretary) and karkoons (clerks); always opened and read his own post, and often wrote his own orders before handing his correspondence to his office.

c 2

Many a mile have we two jogged along the tracks in that part of the country. The only five miles of made road in the district at that time was from Dapoolie to Hurnee, and one could hardly do more than six miles an hour. Colt stopped and talked to every knot of wayfarers we caught up; as I subsequently remembered, was particularly conversational with those who seemed to be pensioned sepoys on their way to the quarterly payment. Their story was always much to the same effect: "It is a good and kind Sirkar (Government). Our pensions are liberal, and we should be content, but the sowkar (money-lender) eats us up, and the Sirkar is blind and helpless." On one occasion I was staying with Colt in the Assistant Collector's picturesque bungalow at Hurnee; there are, by the way, few more beautiful views than that from the spacious verandah. The post was brought up, and Colt, in his armchair, proceeded to open the various packets, sorting and noting on them from time to time. "Hullo," he said suddenly, "here's an anonymous petition saying that a pensioned Jemedar died seven years ago, and that his pension is still drawn by the village headman."

We discussed a little what ought to be done with it, and finally the sheristedar (head clerk) was sent for. He was not shown the petition, but simply asked what was the usual practice in regard to petitions about military pensions, and promptly replied that they should be sent with an endorsement in English by the Saheb to the Paymaster Saheb for the latter's disposal.

Colt seemed to acquiesce, and I quite understood that he had passed on the petition to Dapoolie in accordance with the usual routine.

More than a year passed, and Colt, whose children were ailing, obtained permission to pass the monsoon or rainy months at Dapoolie, instead of at Rutnagiri, the civil headquarters at which I, in common with all other civil officers, was doomed to stay. An old friend of Colt's, the Medical Superintendent of vaccination, accompanied him, and they took a house together. About the middle of the rainy season, Colt wrote to me privately to send him the two most reliable and intelligent men under me, and to let it seem as if the order originated from myself, and was merely a transfer to and from his own usual police guard. At the same time the Magistrate took an opportunity privately of requesting me to give Colt any aid he might ask for, but to keep my own counsel, as there was something serious afoot. Of course I complied, and for two or three months more daily looked out for some stirring news from Dapoolie to relieve the horrible monotony of our daily life.

At last, one evening late in October, while "the station" was assembled and trying to kill time at the daily croquet squabble, the bells of a "dak" runner were heard approaching—obviously an "Ixprèsh," for the regular post was long in. Fearing it might be news of a murder or dacoity, I rushed off to the post-office and found one much-sealed packet addressed in Colt's hand to the

Magistrate, who soon sent for me to request me to transfer a dozen police to Hurnee to obey Colt's orders. He then showed me that officer's confidential despatch, and I made a copy of it for him, and also of a letter which he then and there wrote to the Chief Secretary to Government, enclosing the former, suggesting that a military court of inquiry should assemble at Dapoolie as soon as the "coast opened" for native craft, and that Colt should be nominated to prosecute.

Colt's report was most sensational. It appeared that for nearly two years he had been secretly collecting evidence which showed that, not only had the pensions of deceased pensioners been drawn after their deaths, but that there was an organised conspiracy between "sowkars," or money-lenders, on the one hand, and the Purbhu clerks of the Pension Pay Office on the other, by which pensioned sepoys, and the pensioned families of sepoys perished in service, had been systematically robbed of their pensions for a long series of years. The descriptive rolls of the unfortunates—without which they could not claim payment—were pledged wholesale to money-lenders, who, with the connivance of the clerks, sent up dummies to personate the pensioners and draw their pay, which was every evening brought to the head clerk's office, and there distributed among the sowkars, who let their miserable victims have a few rupees to carry on with till the next pay day.

Colt had actually arrested two of these dummies

with many pensioners' rolls and the full pensions on their persons: he had also seized the account-books for two years of the leading sowkars for three miles round, and found abundant corroborative evidence in them. He had removed the three personating dummies to Hurnee in close custody, and they had already made a clean breast of it, and disclosed ramifications of the plot of the extent of which he himself was not previously aware. Free pardon to these personators, and the prompt suspension from office of the entire military Pension Pay Establishment, was earnestly solicited.

The Magistrate felt, and said, that the arrest and removal of the personators from the limits of the Cantonment without the least communication with the Bazaar-master, as also the seizure of the sowkar's books, might be regarded by higher authorities as a very irregular, high-handed, if not illegal proceeding. On the other hand, it was not to be forgotten that for some few years the military authority in the cantonment of Dapoolie had been notoriously lax, and was certainly ill-defined, and he believed Colt would be able to justify whatever irregularities he might have committed. He would therefore strenuously support him at every point. The Government in the Secret Department (Sir Henry Anderson being Secretary) supported him also, and the military authorities were invited to convene a Court of Inquiry and to suspend the Pay Establishment; pensioners to be paid in the interval by civil agency.

After weeks of harassing delay, which Colt utilised in collecting and arranging his evidence, and the pay clerks devoted to sending daily scurrilous memorials and petitions, anonymous and otherwise, to Government, a "General Order" appeared appointing a Court of Inquiry to assemble at Dapoolie to conduct an investigation into matters which would there be officially communicated to them. The Military Department "saw no present reason for suspending the pension pay subordinates!" The Civil Government authorised a free pardon to the personators. Of the three officers nominated to the Court, the President was at Belgaum, another member in Guzerat, and the third at Ahmednugger, and it was nearly Christmas before the Court could assemble. The details of their proceedings and other explanatory matter must be reserved for another chapter.

CHAPTER III.

THE GREAT MILITARY PENSION FRAUDS—*continued.*

PART II.

LONG before the military court of inquiry could assemble at Dapoolie I had an opportunity of seeing my friend Colt, and hearing from his own mouth, and from his friend the vaccinating Doctor, the details of the grand *coup* by which the conspiracy had been at last exploded.

I was surprised to learn that Colt had not even then taken any steps towards ascertaining the truth of the anonymous letter (to which I have before referred) alleging the fraudulent drawing of a deceased pensioner's pay: he proposed to reserve this particular case for the Court. A less wary man would have worked upon this information from the outset, and thereby, as I easily perceived afterwards, have put the conspirators on their guard.

"Had I," said Colt, "followed the regular routine and sent the petition to the pension paymaster for disposal, it would probably have been so arranged that proof of the fraud would have been difficult— worse still, the office might have brought the case forward as a discovery by themselves, and made capital out of it before the Court. If, on the other hand, I, as Magistrate, had instituted an independent inquiry, the office would have taken alarm, and guessed that I suspected them generally, and would have had ample time and opportunity to 'square' or warn every one all round. It was wiser to let them remain undisturbed in blissful ignorance, impressed with the belief that the new Assistant Collector took no more interest than his predecessors in pensioners or their affairs. It doesn't do to rush your fence, old fellow! So I've left that particular case untouched, and have all this time been picking up what information I could get on other matters more nearly concerning living pensioners and their wrongs. The dead man's case, if it turns out true (as I believe it will), will be a *bonne bouche* for the Court to start upon, and will strengthen my position before them at the outset."

Colt had derived most of his information from two persons to whom I should certainly never have resorted myself: a retired European Conductor of the Ordnance Department, and a young Parsee shopkeeper—about the last people I should have expected to find versed in Hindoo life, or to be able or willing to impart information worth having. Mr. Daniel Monk, the retired Conductor aforesaid, had been for some years settled in a small village a few miles from Dapoolie, where he had leased a few acres of rough land, built himself a small hut, and gone in for coffee growing, more for amusement than with a view to profit. He lived a most secluded life, with one old Mahommedan who had been a quarter of a century in his service.

Domestic trouble in earlier days was supposed to have driven him to the life of a recluse: but, though I knew him as well as any one in those parts, I could never induce him to speak of, or even to refer to, the past.

He rarely left the village; he hardly set foot outside his garden more than twice a year, when he had to get a life certificate to enable him to draw his small annuity: but he was much visited by all classes of natives, who held him in high respect for his blameless life, and perhaps entertained some superstitious regard for him because of his fakir-like habits. Somehow or other, he had taught himself enough Mahratti to be able to read native newspapers, but he took no interest whatever in the current events that interest Europeans; he was, above all, a peacemaker, and many a foolish quarrel was referred to him and settled at his little hut, where he might be seen any day from the road, seated in his verandah or pottering about among his coffee trees. A grand old fellow, past sixty years of age when I knew him, six feet two in height, and as straight as a dart, invariably clad in a loose striped cotton blouse, pyjamas, native sandals, and no stockings.

I have been led to describe him, because he subsequently played an important part in another matter. "But that's another story," as Kipling says! Living this life, he had come to know many of the native pensioners; and his old servant—who, I verily believe, thought he was a saint—brought many of them to him with their troubles.

Fulloo was the son of an old Parsee shopkeeper, who supplied the few European officers in Dapoolie with "Europe stores," and the richer native pensioners with British brandies and other poisons. A very intelligent young fellow of twenty-five was Fulloo, extremely energetic and pushing—as all his people are—and very popular with European and native alike. I am much afraid, however, that Colt would have got very little assistance out of Fulloo, if Fulloo's bibulous customers among the pensioners had paid their little accounts regularly : but the conspirators who robbed them, in their greed left the men barely sufficient to live upon, and were foolish enough not to let Fulloo's bills be regarded as a first claim on their pensions. So Fulloo naturally hated the usurers and the office purbhus (clerks), and was ready enough to impart all he knew—and perhaps a little more—to Colt, to whom, however, he subsequently proved a most valuable agent.

I must here briefly describe, for the information of uninitiated readers, the process of pension payment as it then existed and probably still exists. It was simplicity itself. On being admitted to pension, each man or woman was carefully examined, and a descriptive roll drawn up containing minute details as to age, height, any distinctive marks or scars, general appearance, and so forth. A copy of this document, showing the monthly amount payable, and

DAPOOLIE: PAYING THE PENSIONERS.

[To face p. 29

where payable, was then handed to the pensioner in a neat tin case, with instructions to present it each quarter to the Pension Paymaster. In his office it ought to have remained for a day at most for comparison with the register, then the pensioner's name was called out, and on his answering to it the Pension Paymaster was bound to compare the claimant with his descriptive roll, and then to pay him the quarter's pension in arrears, endorsing on the back of the roll the date and amount paid; the roll was then returned to the pensioner. It was expressly forbidden by general orders that the pensioner should transfer, or by sale or mortgage, part with his descriptive roll. The roll of a deceased pensioner was, or should have been, returned by the village officers to the Pension Pay Office with a report of the death. Nothing could be simpler, nothing could be more perfect as a system, to secure the pensioner getting his pension himself, or to protect the Government against fraud, *provided* the Pension Paymaster rigorously adhered to his orders, and did what he certified on honour every quarter he had done, viz. : *compared each pensioner with his descriptive roll at the time of payment.*

But this comparison was a tedious and troublesome business, and the certificate " on honour" came to be regarded as a form. From a comparison of only a percentage, it at last became the rule to compare none of the pensioners with their rolls; and a large majority of the pensioners, ignorant and improvident as they mostly are, habitually pledged their rolls with the money-lenders for cash advances. The pensioner, at any rate, could not draw his pension without producing his roll, and it was not given to him till the sowkar or usurer, had got a fresh bond out of him up to date. Even then the sowkar usually accompanied his client to the Pay Office, and sat outside—armed with a decree of attachment, in most cases—till the victim came out with his roll and money.

But there were many usurers who would not even trust their clients so far as this, but refused to let the rolls pass again into the hands of their pensioner debtors. Thus a system of dummy pensioners grew up with the connivance of the clerks of the Pay Office, who, of course, were regularly remunerated by the usurers, or not unfrequently had shares in the loans. The usurers then privately handed over their clients' rolls to the clerks, and on an appointed day dummies deputed by the usurers went up, answered to the clients' names, drew the money, received the rolls, and handed the whole (money and rolls) to the usurer at the end of the day's work. It may easily be conceived how completely an indebted pensioner was at the mercy of his creditor, how great was the facility and temptation to the office clerks in the case of deceased pensioners.

Having mastered the outlines of the nefarious conspiracy, Colt's main object was to get at the dummies, to catch them in the very act, with pensions and descriptive rolls on their persons. It was with this object that he settled himself down at

Dapoolie in the monsoon with his friend the doctor, in a bungalow, only separated from the office and residence of the paymaster by a public road; these houses, like all the officers' houses in the station, stood round the edge of and faced the little parade-ground. The brook "Jog" ran behind them, so that persons with information had easy access along its rocky bank to Colt's office without being seen by the assembled pensioners and usurers, or by the clerks in the Pay Office.

About a hundred yards off, on the parade-ground, stood the old quarter-guard, where the treasure needed for payment was kept. From it every morning a little procession of clerks, with two or three pensioners carrying bags of money, wended its way to the Pay Office, and from the office a similar little procession returned every evening with the unexpended balance. Colt soon learnt that the principal dummy was one Tannak, and that he was commonly employed to carry the treasure to and fro. It was some weeks, however, before reliable information was brought by Fulloo that certain large pensions were to be drawn by him.

At last one evening Fulloo rushed in from the brook, and reported that Tannak had drawn three heavy pensions, and that another dummy had drawn others, and that they probably had both the cash and descriptive rolls on them. Colt and the doctor had just time to issue certain orders to his own police and to ensconce themselves behind the garden hedge, when the little procession emerged from the Pay

Office, Tannak leading, loaded with one bag of coin, a pensioner carrying another, the treasurer and another clerk and a peon bringing up the rear. Allowing them just time to enter the quarter-guard, Colt and the doctor raced to the door, entered and shut it, and Colt, turning to Tannak, said, " Tannak, I take you prisoner ! You have just drawn the pensions of Subedar-Major Ramnàk, Jemedar Babaji, and Rowji Naique, and you have the money and the descriptive rolls in your waist-cloth ! "

Without a word, but in abject terror, Tannak produced what he was taxed with, saying, " The sowkars and the clerks have taught me." A similar formality with similar results was gone through with the pensioner dummy, who had two pensions and rolls on his person. Not a word was said to the clerks, who were speechless with fright. The two prisoners were at once escorted by Colt and the doctor to the limits of the cantonment, and handed over to Colt's own police guard, which he had ordered out for the purpose, who conveyed them in a cart to the lock-up at Hurnee. Colt then went to five or six usurers' houses in small villages adjoining the camp and secured their account-books, which he at once took off to Hurnee for minute examination. It was certainly very neatly managed.

The two dummies were, of course, set at liberty directly Colt received Government sanction to their being made approvers. Of the old fellow arrested with Tannak, and three other pensioners similarly employed from time to time, who subsequently gave evidence before the Court of Inquiry, it is unnecessary to speak further; but Tannak merits special description.

Tannak was the son of an old Subedar-Major, who had distinguished himself at the brilliant little battle of Koregaum, and in his old age had settled down at Dapoolie with a special pension. There, in the Mhars' quarter, he built himself a good stone house, buying the occupancy right of a few acres of good land in the vicinity. He brought up his son for the army, and Tannak was duly drilled in the "juvenile squad" up to the age of sixteen, when he so lamed himself in an accident that he could not be enlisted, and after his father's death he had to live as best he could on the family acres. Needless to say, they were soon mortgaged to a usurer in the neighbourhood, who employed him for many years in his transactions with low-caste clients, process serving, executions, and the like.

A fine-looking fellow, well set up and drilled, with a certain military smartness about him, Tannak was unusually intelligent, and, having miraculously abstained from drink, was always trustworthy. So it came to pass when he grew older that he was employed, first by his own usurer, then by others, and finally by usurers and office clerks together, as their most reliable agent at pay time, when he comported himself exactly like a pensioned sepoy, and no ordinary observer would have believed but that he was one. The man was full of humour, and made us almost die of laughing when he related his ex-

D

periences, and acted over and over again how he used to go up and salute the Paymaster sahib, and say "Hazzur"* to any particular name called out for

TANNAK.

which he was to answer. He rarely drew *more* than *two* pensions in one day (!), one in the morning and one in the afternoon, lest the sahib might remember him; but on special occasions, such as that on which

* Present.

he was arrested, he had drawn as many as five, making some slight alteration in his dress and voice, and manner generally. The man was, in fact, a born actor, and thoroughly entered into the fun of the thing. He thought it a great compliment that he was always told off to personate the pensioners of high rank, and was quite proud of having drawn the pension and special allowance of Subedar-Major and Sirdar Bahadur Ramnàk for four years without intermission.

He described to us with great drollery the nocturnal meetings of usurers, clerks, and defrauded pensioners. He, canny man, neither gave up cash nor rolls till he had received his own little commission down, ten, fifteen, or even twenty rupees, and then he would try to get better terms for the poor pensioners concerned, and had even threatened to split if enough money were not doled out to each to carry him on to next quarter-day. He was thus a personage of no small importance and influence in the neighbourhood, and did Colt right good service when the Court was sitting. I afterwards employed him regularly as a secret detective. He never failed me, entering *con amore* into any matter confided to him, and on more than one occasion displaying remarkable detective ability.

To proceed with my tale. When Colt knew that the sealed orders for the Court had arrived at Dapoolie, he took Tannak back with him, and, much more confident in his staunchness than I must confess I was, let him run loose, as it were, among his old associates. Of course, both sowkars and office clerks did their utmost to corrupt him, and to induce him to throw Colt over before the Court. Tannak heard all they had to say, and held out vague hopes, but he never really wavered, and soon furnished Colt with a very valuable piece of information.

The sealed orders came in a large packet addressed "To the President of the Court of Inquiry convened under General order No. so-and-so—*to await arrival.*" The post-master, a Purbhu,* ought, of course, to have kept it in his own charge till the President's arrival, but he chose to deliver it to the Bazaar-master, who, very imprudently—not to say improperly—retained it in his drawer, where it was accessible to his clerks, all bosom-friends of the Pay Office clerks. Tannak had not been a week back at Dapoolie when he informed Colt that by some means or other they had got a copy of the orders, and were busily engaged in devising means to meet Colt's charges by influencing certain witnesses whose names were mentioned.

The first arrival was Waller, the junior member of the Court, a very clever young fellow and an excellent Mahratti scholar, who subsequently earned the Victoria Cross, and rose before his death to high position in the Political Department. He had not the remotest idea what the subject for inquiry was, and must have had rather a dull time of it for a week or so; being impecunious after his long journey, as any subaltern would be, he suffered no little dis-

* Purbhus by caste are almost always clerks or writers by profession.

comfort, for he saw the danger and impropriety of borrowing from any one on the spot.

The fact, however, that he *was* very hard up was soon made known in the bazaar, and Fulloo's first important service was to tell Colt that it had been arranged by the conspirators that one of the chief peccant usurers was to call on him one evening and offer him a loan. Colt thereupon wrote him a confidential note warning him of the coming visit, and to be on his guard against all and sundry. The lieutenant in due course wrote that the visit and proposal had duly come off, and that he should report the incident to the President, as he afterwards did.

The President and second member of the Court arrived nearly together, and no time was lost in convening the first meeting. The selection of the Court did great credit to the judgment of Headquarters. The President, a brevet-colonel of no small personal experience of military courts-martial, had a sufficient colloquial knowledge of the vernacular, and though somewhat brusque and hasty, was remarkably quick of observation, and the incarnation of fairness. Captain Bird, the second member, had long been adjutant of his regiment, and was an unusually good Mahratti scholar, besides being an excellent accountant. The members were nearly strangers to each other, and complete strangers to the Pension Paymaster and to Colt.

At the preliminary meeting the President, after a short address, produced the sealed packet of orders, together with an official letter from the Bazaar-master, reporting that it had been handed to him (the President) by the Bazaar-master. He was about to open it when Colt rose and deferentially requested that it should be first inspected, and its appearance and condition noted. The President could not suppress a look of angry surprise towards Colt, a sort of "you d——d cheeky young civilian" kind of a look, but, controlling himself, said: "Well, gentlemen, there's no harm in *that*." And proceeding to inspect the seals before passing the packet round, ejaculated, "My God! gentlemen, it has been tampered with!" And so it evidently had; by some means—probably with the heated blade of a knife—the seals had been evidently raised, and re-set, *but* the paper under the seals had been cut! Tableau! Marked change in the manner of the President to Colt the prosecutor. Bazaar-master and post-master summoned to the Court. Packet carefully cut open and contents read, while the Court awaited the arrival of the two officials. The junior member produces correspondence with Colt, and reports the loan incident. Rough notes of proceedings drawn up, and the Pension Paymaster summoned to appear forthwith with all his office establishment.

Meantime arrives the post-master, who states that he handed the packet to the Bazaar-master, as being the chief military officer at Dapoolie. The seals were then intact, and did not bear their present appearance. The Bazaar-master, by no means a "master mind," says he received the sealed packet from the post-master, though it was not addressed to his care; thought it was all right; did not think of examining the seals; put the packet in his office drawer; does not always lock his office drawer, but is *quite* sure none of *his* establishment would dare to look into it! President, dismissing him, observes briefly that the facts will be forthwith reported to army headquarters.* Then enters the Pension Paymaster, with some eight or ten clerks and a couple of peons. The contents of the sealed packet are read out to them, and they request that a copy may be supplied to them. The Paymaster is warned to keep his office papers under lock and key, and told that he will be informed when his own presence or that of his clerks is required.

The President, inviting Colt to remain for consultation, declared that he had been much impressed by the incident of the tampered-with seals, and resolved that it be forthwith reported to army headquarters. Colt, meekly observing that he had excellent reasons for suspecting foul play, ventured to put in a letter asking, for reasons stated, that the Court should also recommend the immediate suspension of the entire Pension Pay Establishment, and the transfer of all its records, and, temporarily, of all its duties, to the Court itself. Considerable discussion followed. Colt requested to withdraw, was re-called and informed that the Court had decided to adopt his suggestion and to forward his letter. Adjournment *sine die.*

* N.B.—He was promptly retired from the service.

Such is a brief record of the opening day, and it must be admitted that Colt scored heavily. He never would tell me how much he knew about the sealed packet; but I have a shrewd suspicion that from some place of concealment he actually saw the packet opened by the clerks and certain usurers in secret conclave. If so, he must have possessed amazing self-control not to have seized them in the act.

Almost by return of post the President received authority from army headquarters to suspend every one they named and to carry on the Pension Paymaster's duties pending further orders. Captain Bird accordingly took possession of all the office papers, and from this point the inquiry may be said to have begun. The proceedings were from time to time sensational in the extreme, but the account of them will take another chapter.

CHAPTER IV.

THE GREAT MILITARY PENSION FRAUDS—*continued*.

Part III.

AFTER the grand *coup* of the suspension of the entire Pension Pay Department there was a long lull at Dapoolie. The Court of Inquiry were fully occupied in making lists of and taking over the documents in the office, and in mastering the office routine.

My friend Colt went off to the village wherein had resided the deceased pensioner, whose pension—so said the anonymous petition—had been drawn for seven years after his death. The case was a very clear one, and the conspirators, who included the village patel and kulkarni, were duly committed to the sessions; where, I may mention, they were soon after convicted and sentenced to various long terms of imprisonment. There was no direct evidence, however, to support their story that the clerks in the Pay Office were cognizant of, and shared in, the plunder, but Colt had no doubt this was so.

In due course the Court reassembled, and Colt opened his case, first of all by putting in copies of the proceedings in the deceased pensioner's case just referred to. He then called his best witness in his strongest case, that of Subedar-Major Sirdar Bahadur Ramnàk Bhàgnàk. I have already mentioned that for specially good service he, from one fund and another, received the (to him) magnificent pension of sixty-seven rupees a month, or rather that, with the connivance of the clerk, my friend Tannak drew it regularly for the sowkars, who doled out to him about ten rupees a month! Three of these cormorants had him down in their books for several hundreds of rupees. Every quarter-day he passed a fresh bond to each creditor, and the whole of the sowkar's dealings with him were found carefully recorded in their accounts. The fine old fellow resided in Dapoolie. His appearance was familiar to every one, and his deeds of prowess were common talk. Almost every day he might be seen wending his way across the "maidan," or parade-ground, within a few yards of the Paymaster's office, clad in a long white gaberdine, or night shirt (as we should rather term it in these degenerate days), a long staff in his hand, his beard and fierce-looking white mustachios curled upward and backward, and always accompanied by a child or two. I remember a sketch of Van Ruith's which might have been his portrait. It was truly remarkable that a personage so notable—the head of the pensioners' list—should not have been treated with special honour and consideration, that his absence at each quarterly payment for more than four years should not have attracted the attention of the paymaster; but so it was!

Mr. Colt assured me that his grand soldier-like appearance, his frank demeanour, and the obvious truthfulness with which he gave his evidence had as powerful an effect on the Court as he himself calculated upon.

Colt then proceeded to call over a hundred witnesses in dozens of similar cases, and could have gone on for months, but that the President declared that the Court was satisfied. A short report of progress was then made to army headquarters, and permission was asked for and obtained for the Court to adjourn to Chiploon, another important paying station. A few more important cases were picked up there, and then the Court returned to Dapoolie, and prepared and sent in a voluminous report. They were promptly instructed to supply the Paymaster and the clerks with a copy of it, and to call upon them for any explanation they might desire to give.

The Paymaster elected to appear personally before the Court; his subordinates promised to submit a joint written defence. In due course the Paymaster appeared, and the pith of his argument was, that in the twenty years he had performed the duties, he had no doubt that laxity had crept in, but that he was confident in the rectitude of his clerks, whom he vehemently declared to be maligned individuals.

Asked by the President if he habitually compared each applicant for payment of his pension with his description roll, he was forced to admit that he had not done so for some years, as his experience was so great that he was confident he could detect personation at a glance.

Asked how he reconciled it with his duty to sign at the foot of the quarterly list of payments the certificate, "I hereby certify on my honour that at the time of payment I duly compared each pensioner with his descriptive roll," the poor old gentleman said that he had regarded this as a mere form; and he insisted again and again that he never could be deceived, but should instantly detect any personator.

At this moment the President, after consulting with his colleagues, passed a pencilled note over to Colt: "Call Tannak in quietly from behind." Now Tannak was always kept handy at the stable. Colt slipped out and told Tannak to go round and come up to the front door just as he did when drawing pensions. In a few minutes Tannak appeared at the threshold, and, drawing himself up, delivered himself of a military salute, ejaculating, "Saheb! Meri urzee hai" (I have a petition to make).

Quoth the President, "Major, look at that man! Is he a pensioner?"

"Certainly he is," replied the major. "I am quite familiar with his appearance."

"Doubtless you are, sir," drily remarked the President. "This man is Tannak, who has often personated pensioners, and drawn four and five pensions in a single day."

Tableau! in the midst of which the poor old paymaster drifted away, and Tannak, saluting, returned to his stable.

After numerous and at last peremptory messages, the clerks came to the Court with a document purporting to be their defence. It consisted mainly of gross abuse of Colt, the prosecutor, enlarged on a few discrepancies in the evidence, and announced their intention of prosecuting Colt for suborning evidence.

Asked if that was all they had to say, they replied in the affirmative, but expressed a hope that the Court would receive any further statement they might be able to make. The President said that it would take the Court ten days to prepare their report to headquarters, and that they would receive anything tendered on or before the tenth day, when the doors would be closed, and the prosecutor himself would leave the neighbourhood on other urgent duty.

Colt thought he observed the clerks rather prick up their ears at the latter piece of news, and determined not to relax his vigilance in the interim— and he was repaid. The ten days slipped away without a sign from the clerks, and Colt made his arrangements for a long march on the eleventh day. The evening before, he was walking down the bazaar, when he came upon one of the petty sowkars whose books had not been seized at the outset, but who had been casually mentioned in the course of the inquiry. The man was walking briskly and somewhat jauntily along, but on meeting Colt he was visibly disconcerted. Colt could not understand what it meant, and for the time dismissed the matter from his mind. Very early in the morning, however, he was awakened by the Parsi informer Fulloo's voice at his bedside in the old deserted bungalow in which he slept. "Saheb! Saheb! get up. The clerks have some 'daga' (treachery) afoot; they've had a meeting with Dewchund Shroff." Now Dewchund was the very man Colt had met and disconcerted on the previous evening!

After some palaver with Fulloo, Colt decided only to pretend to go, and to make his way back to Dapoolie by eleven o'clock. Accordingly "chota hazri" (early breakfast) was taken as usual, and the remaining kit sent off, and about seven o'clock Colt cantered round the "maidan" and took a cordial farewell of the members of the Court, and then started ostensibly on the march. Four or five miles off he turned back, and, knowing the ground well, made his way round by a "nullah" to the back of his old house, stabled his "tat," and from a clump of bushes watched the entrance to the court's office.

About half-past ten he perceived a procession of spotlessly-dressed clerks filing into the court's compound or garden; and shortly afterwards, being sure that they were before the Court, he walked quietly down, and entering by a side gate Colt was in the court-room before the clerks (who were seated in a semicircle with their backs to him) could perceive him.

"Hullo!" shouted the President. "What—not gone yet?"

"No," said Colt quietly. "I thought I'd just see it out to-day."

"Well, Mr. Prosecutor," quoth the President, "your

presence is most opportune, for the accused have just brought us a letter which they say contains matter of serious import to them, and we may as well go into it at once." The discomfiture of the clerks, Colt told me, was ludicrous—they would have given anything to have got the letter back, but the President had it, opened it, and at once began to read it.

Now, one of the class of cases Colt had produced related to the swindling of female pensioners who received some small quarterly allowance from the State because their husbands had been killed in action, or for some kindred reason. They too had pledged their descriptive rolls with sowkars, and many of them had never received an anna for years. One Cassee, for instance, entitled to two rupees a month, or six rupees per quarter, had left her roll with a leading sowcar, and gone to service in Poona with the family of the Bazaar-master there. For seven years or more she had never left Poona, and Colt proved it, and showed that her pension had all the time been drawn in Dapoolie by sowcars. It was a strong case, and one that had particularly aroused the indignation of the Court at the time.

The clerks' petition related to this case. They said that they had just accidentally discovered a most important piece of evidence, which would at once break down this case, and the Court would then easily see how Mr. Colt must have fabricated most of the other evidence against them. The evidence lay in the testimony of one Dewchund Shroff, who had dealings with Cassee, and would produce his books, to show that on several occasions during eighteen months of her supposed absence at Poona, she *must* have been in Dapoolie and paid small instalments in person; they therefore prayed instant inquiry, and that Dewchund might be summoned to bring his books.

The Court agreed, and sent off the summons to Dewchund, who lived quite close, Colt merely requested that no one of the accused should leave the court-room till Dewchund arrived. This was granted, and the Court sat in solemn silence for about half-an-hour, when Dewchund was seen walking with all his old jauntiness up the carriage-drive, some red-covered account-books under his arm. Entering the room, however, he caught sight of Colt, and simply collapsed!

The President called upon the head pension clerk to examine Dewchund, and with abject misery depicted in his countenance the former went through the preconcerted lesson.

" Do you know one Cassee Kom Nagoo ? "

" Yes, I do."

" Have you had money dealings with her ? "

" Yes."

" When has she paid you money with her own hand ? "

" I will look at my books and tell you." Books reluctantly untied and referred to by Dewchund. " She paid me on such a date Rs. 2, on another date Rs. 2 'hasta Khood,' with her own hand."

Books thereupon handed round to the Court, and extracts taken in silence.

Clerks and Dewchund evidently more chirpy, but Court glum, and looking coldly at Colt, who merely said, "Will the Court permit me to see those books?" "Certainly," says the President in his iciest manner.

Now Colt had been for some time a special officer of income-tax; he read Guzerati well, and was thoroughly up in all matters relating to native account-books. After a moment's inspection he quietly handed them back to the President, remarking—

"I demand that these books be impounded, and I take Dewchund in custody. These books have been tampered with! The leaves containing the entries have been interpolated."

Great excitement in the Court. The President observing, "Take care, sir; this is a most serious accusation you make, and it should be substantiated at once."

To which Colt replied—

"Let these miserable men—look at them, gentlemen!—let them nominate a member of a panchayet, or Jury, let the Court nominate another, and myself a third, and I agree to abide by their award."

No sooner said than done, and the panchayet in due course assembled. Colt's quick eye had detected one sufficient flaw which convinced him that a panchayet would find many more.

Native account-books are made of native paper, cut

E

with a sharp knife, like that of a shoemaker, from reams of paper in which there is usually a crease in folding. Every leaf cut, of course, has the same crease, and Colt instantly noticed that the leaves on which Cassee's items were endorsed had a different crease from the rest of the book, and therefore must have been recently sewn in. He also noticed that though there were entries for past years, checked at the Dewali item by item, when a small circular mark like the letter O is made at the left-hand of each item, there were no such marks on these particular pages!

To cut a long story short, the panchayet unanimously, by these and other details, pronounced the entries to be false. Colt took possession of Dewchund, the clerks sneaked off, and the Court proceeded to relate in the report to headquarters this "grand climax."

In "due course," that is to say, after some months deliberation, orders came down from army headquarters dismissing every soul in the Pension Pay Establishment, from the Paymaster down to the peons. In the then defective state of the criminal law it was found that no one could be prosecuted. I believe military pensioners have since been fairly treated; but so long as men so ignorant have anything—be it a piece of paper, be it a simple token—that they think they can pledge, or that they can be persuaded is pledgable, so long will this villainous extortion exist in a greater or less degree according to the vigilance of the paymaster for the time being.

Colt in due course of time received the high commendations of the Secretary of State, and no one can deny that he merited them. What happened to Dewchund I do not remember. Tannak became a respectable character, and a very useful police informer, and died at a green old age, greatly looked up to by pensioners, and never weary of relating the incidents of the Court of Inquiry, where he boasted that Colt Saheb would have been helpless without him.

At some future time I shall have a story to tell about native account-books and their fabrication; but, following the lines I have laid down, I must next address myself to the topic of undetected murders.

Moral—for those about to begin official life in India —learn to read well and write the vernacular of the district you are serving in. You will be but a belled cat otherwise. Read your own petitions yourself, to yourself, by yourself; act on them with the utmost caution. Keep anonymous letters locked up, and don't speak of them even to your trusty "Sheristedar." Do not "rush your fence" when you do act, or you will find disappointment, and your zeal will be effectually extinguished.

CHAPTER V

BUSSAPA'S REVENGE.

BEFORE recounting the history of another anonymous petition, it will be convenient to relate one more instance of vindictiveness, surpassing, and even more unnatural than that of Vinayek Deo, the "would-be parricide." It occurred in the southern Mahratta country some ten or fifteen years ago, and was duly chronicled in official reports as one of the most remarkable crimes of the year.

When I first knew Bussapa Patel, about 1863, he was as fine and promising a specimen of the young Mahratta as one would wish to see. About twenty years of age, tall for a Mahratta, strongly built, with a particularly frank and intelligent cast of countenance, he was the pride of his old father, Yellapa Patel, one of the most prosperous farmers in the cotton country, who had had him educated in much better style than was then customary among people of his class.

Yellapa, like all cotton growers in that part of the Western Presidency, profited enormously by the high price of the staple during the American war. Silver was poured into the country (literally) in

LES NOUVEAUX RICHES.

[To face p. 63

crores or millions sterling, and cultivators who previously had as much as they could do to live, suddenly found themselves possessed of sums their imaginations had never dreamt of. What to do with their wealth, how to spend their cash, was their problem.

Having laden their women and children with ornaments, and decked them out in expensive sarees (petticoats) they launched into the wildest extravagance in the matter of carts and trotting bullocks, going even as far as silver-plated yokes and harness studded with silver mountings. Even silver tires to the wheels became the fashion. Twelve and fifteen hundred rupees were eagerly paid for a pair of trotting bullocks.* Trotting matches for large stakes were common; and the whole rural population appeared with expensive red silk umbrellas, which an enterprising English firm imported as likely to gratify the general taste for display.

Many took to drink, not country liquor such as had satisfied them previously, but British brandy, rum, gin, and even champagne. Among these last was Yellapa, who was rarely sober during the last few months of his life, having by his example and encouragement made Bussapa a drunkard also.

About the time when Yellapa died the tide of prosperity turned. The American war at an end, down went the price of cotton, and a series of bad seasons set in, culminating with the great famine of 1876-77 and the rat plague. Silver tires, silver

---

* A rupee was then worth 2s. 3d.

ornaments, disappeared from every household, valuable cattle died from drought and disease, or had to be sold for what they would fetch; and every farmer, Bussapa Patel among them, found himself heavily in debt to the village sowkar. Habits of drinking and reckless extravagance contracted during the "cotton mania" were not easily shaken off, and Bussapa went on from bad to worse, became extremely violent in temper when in his cups, and sullen and morose in his sober intervals.

His wife, to whom it was said he was deeply attached, then died, leaving him a fine, bright little boy of about five or six years of age. Little Bhow seemed to be the only thing Bussapa cared for, and he loved to send him out into the village, where he was a great pet, dressed in a little bright crimson jacket, and wearing such silver anklets and bangles as he could still afford to give him.

As may be well imagined, Bussapa's affairs had drifted into a well-nigh hopeless state by the end of the great famine. He had mortgaged all he had, including his "inam," or service land, to the principal banker in the village, and was only able to stagger along with the aid of small advances obtained from time to time from the same source.

Dewchund Shroff was not a bad sort of fellow, as sowkars go; he and his father had had dealings with the Patels for many years, and the families were as intimate as Mahrattas and Wanias can be. Little Bhow was an almost daily visitor at Dewchund's shop, where he was always sure to get some sweetmeat or other little treat dear to childhood. Latterly, indeed, Bhow passed nearly all his time out of school at or near Dewchund's place, for his father Bussapa's drunken violence frightened the little fellow, while Dewchund always made much of him.

Dewchund's relations with Bussapa gradually

BHOW AT DEWCHUND'S SHOP.

became strained; the latter's constant applications for fresh advances, his violence and obstinate refusal to go into his account, or to enter into a new bond, angered Dewchund, whose patience was finally exhausted when he learnt indirectly that Bussapa, instead of dealing exclusively with him, as had hitherto been the understanding between them, had secretly obtained an advance on his coming cotton crop from a merchant at Coompta.

A stormy scene ensued between them, Dewchund taxing Bussapa with breach of faith, Bussapa retorting by vile abuse and threats of what harm he, as Patel, would do to the sowkar. Losing temper altogether, Dewchund at last told Bussapa that if he did not settle up within three days he would file a suit against him without further notice. During the next two days Bussapa drank heavily, and was hardly seen outside his house; but little Bhow, as usual, passed most of his time down at Dewchund's shop.

It afterwards transpired that Dewchund took no steps whatever to carry out his threat, and he always declared that he only uttered it in anger, that for the sake of old friendship he would have been willing to let matters go on as before, if Bussapa would only show himself fair and reasonable.

On the third night after the quarrel, Dewchund's shutters were up, and he was sitting about midnight making up his accounts in his shop, according to custom, when Bussapa knocked at the shutters and demanded admittance. Dewchund let him in, put up the shutters, and, turning round, saw Bussapa mouthing and muttering to himself in a corner. The man's haggard, blazing eyes and suppressed manner frightened Dewchund; he was about to call out, when Bussapa said, "Hold your tongue! I've brought your money. Where is the account?" On this they sat down, Bussapa became seemingly calmer, and Dewchund produced the ledger and quietly made up the total with interest. The usual wrangle followed, but at last Dewchund agreed to knock off a good lump sum of interest, and Bussapa made him bring out the mortgage deed and other bonds, and told him to endorse them as discharged, and, moreover, to write out a receipt in full of all demands.

Dewchund demurred to doing this until he had secured, or at least had seen the money, which he supposed Bussapa carried about him in notes. Bussapa became very indignant at this, and got up, exclaiming, " I am not lying; I've brought the money value. Come and see. I put the bag in your out-buildings."

Rather surprised, and getting much alarmed, Dewchund lit a lantern, and they went into the back yard, Bussapa leading the way to a shed, in one corner of which was a large heap of dried cow-dung cakes, the fuel of the country, which had evidently been just disturbed. There Bussapa, putting down the lantern, suddenly seized Dewchund by the throat with one hand, so that he could not cry out, forced him to the ground, and, in suppressed tones, spoke rapidly into his ear, " You devil, I have paid you with my son's life! I've killed little Bhow, and hidden his body in that heap. If you don't agree to what I say, I'll raise the alarm now, and accuse you of having murdered him for the sake of his ornaments! Quick! If you consent, raise your arm, and then come back with me to the shop."

Stupefied with fear, Dewchund lifted his hand, and Bussapa, still holding him firmly, half led, half dragged him back to the house, where, after again threatening him if he should call out, Bussapa released his hold, and in the same suppressed fierce tone said, "Now you're paid, give me the papers and a receipt." Dewchund so far recovered his presence of mind as to ask what was to be done with the body, and Bussapa replied, "We will take it away, and bury it in the nullah (watercourse) presently." On this Dewchund gave up the papers duly endorsed, with trembling hand wrote out a receipt in full, and then followed Bussapa with the light to the shed.

Bussapa took out the poor little body from the heap of cow-dung, wrapped it in his blanket, and bade Dewchund lead the way to a dry nullah a few hundred yards off, and to carry a shovel with him. There Bussapa dug a deep hole in the loose shingle and buried the body, piling on large stones. It was near daylight when, returning by another route, they reached the confines of the village and separated, Bussapa assuring Dewchund that he need have no fear, as he should accuse some "Kaikarris,"* or basket-makers, then encamped near the village, of the murder.

* "Kaikarris" belong to the predatory tribes; ostensibly they are basket-makers. For a full account of them, see General Hervey's Diary before mentioned.

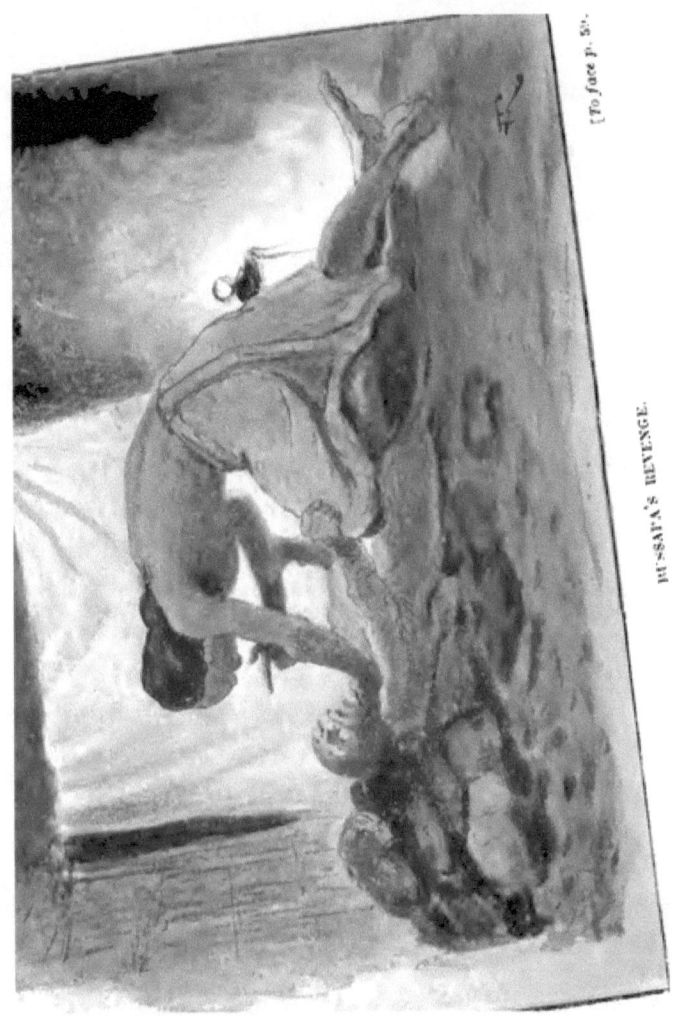

HUSSAFA'S REVENGE.

Dewchund crept home more dead than alive, shivering with terror, and feeling very little confidence in Bussapa's assurance. Bussapa, brooding devilishly over the events of the night, first destroyed all the papers by fire, and then tossing off cup after cup of raw spirit, communed with himself somewhat as follows : " That sowkar devil can't sue and disgrace me now, that's true ; and I now owe nothing, that's good ! But what a price ! How can I live without little Bhow ? Arè ! Arè ! What can I do ? . . . I must give the alarm directly about the little fellow's disappearance. . . . I'll have the Kaikarris' camp searched first . . . I can easily slip little Bhow's ornaments into one of their huts while making search . . . then the body will be found later in the day. . . . But stop a moment ! Why should I let that sowkar devil off after all ? He forced me to kill Bhow. He ought to die. . . ."

Falling at last into a drunken stupor, Bussapa was roused about nine in the morning by a servant asking where was " Bhow Baba," and he acted at once on the evil resolution he had already half formed. Heading a search-party he went from house to house, inquiring and looking in out-buildings, till they got to Dewchund's shop. Dewchund's face and terrified manner were enough to rouse suspicion ; the disturbed heap of cow-dung, the shovel, evidently lately used, added to it ; a neighbour had heard Dewchund returning to his house early in the morning ; a Kaikarri on the prowl had seen him sneaking back to it; there were tracks from the shed leading to the nullah; the nullah was searched, fresh digging found, and the child's body was speedily exhumed.

Dewchund was seized and handed over to the police, and no one doubted that he really had strangled the poor little fellow, taken his ornaments, and disposed of the body in the dead of night. His incoherent protestations, his asseverations that Bussapa had killed his own son, were naturally regarded as the ravings of a detected criminal. The " Punchayat," or Coroner's jury, found that the little boy had been strangled by Dewchund for the sake of his ornaments, and though these were not found in his house, Dewchund was hurried off to jail, and ultimately brought before a magistrate.

With some difficulty a "vakil," or pleader, was found to defend him. Even he for some time placed no credit in the ghastly story Dewchund related, but at last he induced the magistrate to order a search of Bussapa's house, and there, in a bundle of Bussapa's own clothes, the few paltry ornaments were found concealed. Bussapa, in his besotted malignity, had forgotten to take them with him and secrete them in Dewchund's house when the alarm was first given; and the police immediately taking possession of the house, he never found an opportunity of rectifying the omission afterwards.

Kept under strict surveillance after the discovery of the ornaments, and unable to obtain liquor, Bussapa's nerve gave way in a few days, and he made a clean breast of it. Dewchund was released, and in due course Bussapa was arraigned, convicted, and hanged.

To the last his principal regret was that he had not done for Dewchund! And, indeed, had he not, in his bemuddled excitement, forgotten to take the silver anklets with him to Dewchund's house on the day of the latter's arrest, Dewchund would in all human probability have been hanged in his stead. The chain of circumstantial evidence against him lacked but this one link, and the true story of the crime as persisted in by him would have been set aside as utterly incredible.

Bussapa, in his confession, asserted, and no doubt truthfully, that the idea of sacrificing his son never entered his brain till just before he visited Dewchund on the fatal night—that it suddenly flashed across him in his rage and despair what a fine revenge this would be, how easy a release from Dewchund's clutches. The boy was sleeping beside him, was dead in a moment, and he was out on his way to the sowkar's house with the body before he fully realised what he had done. There is a saying, "Revengeful like a Canarese," and this tale hideously illustrates it.

CHAPTER VI.

UNDISCOVERED MURDER, UNPUNISHED MURDER, AND KIDNAPPING.

I CALL to mind three very remarkable instances of undoubted murder, duly reported, which, despite the strong suspicion that there was against certain individuals, had finally to be struck off the register. Every police officer of superior grade must have encountered hundreds of such hard nuts to crack, and had to abandon them after months, or sometimes years, of unremitting watchfulness. Again, however, I maintain that the police are no more to be blamed in India than their much more intelligent and highly-trained *confrères* in England, working among a more civilised population, and are aided by telegraphs and railways in every direction. It is all very well to say "murder will out," but it by no means follows that the murderer *must* be found out. A considerable percentage of murderers always have defied, and always will defy, detection, and if the perpetrators bear the brand of Cain upon their brows, it is invisible to human eyes.

The first instance—which included kidnapping—occurred some twenty-five years ago on the confines of a Mahomedan state near Bombay, where there was a constant demand for concubines among the higher and more powerful Mahomedans. At the time I speak of, and notably in the native state I refer to, the kidnapping of women from adjacent British territory was common. No case, however, has occurred for many years.

Balloo was a strapping young Mahratta residing in a small village on the confines of the state in question. He married almost a child-wife, whom he left with his mother and family while he went to Bombay to seek employment. He got on the G. I. P. Railway, and finally by good conduct was promoted to the post of gatekeeper. All this time he regularly remitted small sums for his wife's expenses, and occasionally received a letter from her written by the village koolkarnee (accountant).

Six months having passed without his having received any news, he became uneasy, and got a letter written to the " patel," or head man, of his village, asking for intelligence. The reply was that his wife was for the time absent from the village on a visit to her own mother, but would return shortly. Balloo did not quite like this, and with some difficulty obtaining leave, set out to go home and bring his wife back with him. Arrived at his village he found his wife absent, and his mother told him that she had been sent for by her mother a couple of months before.

Meantime, Balloo heard in the village an unpleasant rumour that about the time his wife left, a

Mahomedan of some rank from the neighbouring state had visited the village and been entertained for some days by the patel. Balloo interviewed the patel the next morning, who said his wife was coming back that very day, proposed that they should go out to meet her as far as the next village. Now the way to that village ran through some very wild country and densely-wooded ravines. The simple fellow consented and then and there the pair started off. The patel returned in the evening and gave out that Balloo having met his wife had returned with her to her mother's house, and was afterwards going to take her with him to his place on the railway.

No suspicion whatever was excited at the time, for the patel's story was plausible and probable enough; but a few months afterwards, in the hot season, a gowlee (herdsman) came upon a human skeleton in this particular jungle, the skull of which was fractured in pieces. Some half-rotten rags on the bones were identified by his mother as being those that Balloo went away in; she also pointed to a fractured front tooth which Balloo was known to have. Suspicion, of course, fell on the patel, who stoutly denied his guilt, but his former plausible tale was soon proved to be false in every way. Then came out the fact that two or three months before, at about the time the wealthy Mahomedan had visited the village, and Balloo's wife had also disappeared from the scene, the patel had been somewhat flush of cash, had bought cattle,

THE FATAL DELL. [*To face* p. 64.

had paid off debts, and seemed generally in flourishing circumstances.

Inquiries were then set on foot in the neighbouring state through the Political Agent, who employed Bombay detectives; who, after incredible difficulty, ascertained that Balloo's wife was living as one of the concubines of the Nawab's own uncle.

The greatest difficulties were, of course, thrown in our way by the Nawab's "durbar,"* so that when the patel was tried before the sessions, the Judge felt justified in receiving secondary evidence of Balloo's wife being alive and of where she was. Not a single reliable witness, however, could be obtained from the Native State! The Judge convicted the patel, but the "Sudder," or high court, reversed the conviction. The Judge, however, addressed a letter to the Government, recounting the circumstances, and there being several other serious matters pending against the same Nawab, Government took vigorous steps, which resulted not only in the restoration of Balloo's wife to her family, but in the release of some two hundred other women similarly kidnapped from British territory or brought over from Zanzibar.

It subsequently came out pretty clearly that the patel received some three hundred rupees from the agent of the then Nawab's uncle for kidnapping Balloo's wife. No doubt he counted on Balloo's staying away till there should be time for it to be rumoured with some plausibility that the girl had gone off of her own accord. Balloo's return and his

---

* Executive officer of the State.

pertinacity drove the patel to desperation, so he knocked poor Balloo on the head at the first suitable spot they came to during their last walk. This, however, is conjecture. In this particular case, at any rate, the police did their level best, and I remember at the time I thought, with the Judge, that they deserved considerable credit.

The Marwari Mystery.

The second case of undiscovered murder that I shall relate can be very briefly told. In a certain village there resided an old Marwari money-lender, believed to be very wealthy, and nearly every farmer near was in his books. He had a deed-box of bulky dimensions, visible to every one from the outer shop. Cash or notes he could produce to any amount, but he brought them from a secret hiding-place, known to no one, in an inner chamber. He slept in that room, which was the corner room of his adobe-built house. A greater skinflint and a more offensive old villain never lived. He possessed no friends, and every creditor far and near detested him.

His grand-daughter, a widow of about twenty-five, kept house for him. She slept in the corner room of the opposite side of his house. Two men (Purdèsees) as his private guard slept in an out-house adjacent. One midnight, the grand-daughter, hearing some noise from the old man's room, lit an oil light, and was about to enter his bed-room, when the door opened and her grandfather appeared, blood pouring from his mouth and nostrils, his eyes protruding; he fell right on to her, extinguishing the light. The Purdèsees rushed in just in time to hear their master utter a few inarticulate sounds, before he died.

There was a police post about three miles off, so the police were quickly on the spot. It was found that a hole had been made in the adobe wall near the old man's bed large enough to admit the passage of a man. There were no signs of a struggle, except that the old man's mattress was saturated with blood. A trap-door in the floor was still locked, and when opened, the old man's bags of rupees, a tin box containing a large sum in currency notes, and a bundle of jewellery of considerable value were revealed. Nothing had been touched, and the deed-box was also unopened.

The post-mortem examination showed that the poor wretch had been partially smothered, and that by the knees of his assailant his ribs were mostly fractured and violently forced into his lungs; the wonder was how he could ever have risen again. Not the faintest clue was obtained. He was at enmity with all and every one, but no particular individuals had a special grudge against him. There was nothing to show that robbery had been intended.

The police took possession of the house, filled up the hole in the wall, and then took up their abode in the place, carefully avoiding, however, the old man's room. They had been there some fourteen days when the room was entered in precisely the same manner and place, disgusting evidence of the entry being left behind. Intense personal hatred was, in my opinion, the motive for the crime, but no trace whatever of the criminals was discovered, nor was any one even suspected. The police, of course, who were grievously to blame in not detecting the second entry, were severely punished for their negligence.

Murder, Suicide, or Accident?

The third and last doubtful case I shall narrate, though it was generally believed to have been a murder, may, I have always thought, have been an accident or a suicide. It was a peculiar case, because two Europeans were dragged into it.

I was at the well-known fair-weather port Hurnee down the coast, when about eleven in the morning, while the tide was running out, leaving here and there patches of rock more or less exposed along the shore, when news was brought to me that the body of a woman had just been washed up on to a rock plateau under the Severndroog Fort, in which were the headquarters of the sub-district.*

It was hardly a mile from my tent. Hastening to the spot, I found the body of a fine young woman,

---

* There are, or rather were, five forts close to each other. The two principal ones can only be seen from the point selected by my artist, which is close to the tomb of Tuláji Angria.

SEVERNDROOG, ALSO KNOWN AS HURNEE, FROM THE TOMB OF TULAJI ANGRIA.

[To face p. 63.

nude, except as to the breast-cloth, which was rucked up under the arms by the wash of the waves. The people had just found her "sarree," or petticoat, caught on the rocks, which showed her to be a Mahomedan. The body was quite fresh, and she clearly had not been dead more than an hour or two. There was only one serious injury observable,— a severe contused wound on her temple, which had evidently bled considerably; there were also scratches all over the body, probably caused after death by the body tossing about among the barnacle-covered rocks.

The usual "punchayet," or jury, had already made their report—that the woman had been murdered by some person or persons unknown. I, however, promptly sent the body up to the Civil Hospital, which happened to be some eight miles distant, at Dapoolie. In due course I received a report that the wound on the head, though not of itself sufficient to cause death, had probably stunned the woman, causing her to fall into the water, or that her head had struck a rock in falling, and she had been drowned while unconscious. There was no other cause of death, and the woman, the doctor said, had probably died about six or seven in the morning.

She had been immediately identified as the wife— the erring wife—of an absent fisherman, and had been seen making her way over the jagged boulders of the rocky groin I have spoken of, about six o'clock that morning, carrying with her the kind of creel which native women use when picking shell-fish off the rocks. The little port was full of "pattimars" (native craft), by which, in those days, the whole traffic, goods and passenger, of the coast was worked. It was blowing a stiff north-wester, and all the craft lay at anchor under a headland near.

I was just settling down to work, after return to camp, when an excited crowd approached. In the midst of it walked two very irate Europeans. Of course the cry was that these two "soldier lôk" having first ravished the woman, had then thrown her into the sea. With some difficulty I cleared the neighbourhood, and was able to interrogate the two men. One of them was an army schoolmaster travelling up to a new situation beyond Bombay; the other was a sergeant who had served for his pension. The papers in each case were in order; they were sailing up at Government expense, and were to all appearance as decent fellows as one could wish to meet.

They said that, as the tindal (native captain) of their "pattimar" told them that they could not proceed in the face of the north-wester, they had got him to land them in the ship's small boat, so that they might get a little exercise. The headland was about two miles off, and it was easy to send for the tindal to ascertain at what hour he had put them ashore; meantime I examined their clothes carefully for blood-stains, but found none.

The tindal deposed that he had landed them about 10.30 A.M. at the headland, two miles distant, so that they clearly could never have seen the woman who was found dead before 8 A.M. Native malice, however, insisted on their guilt, the nearest Mahratta newspaper in its next issue accused me of hushing up the matter, while half-a-dozen anonymous letters were sent to Government accusing me of all kinds of crimes!

I stayed some time in the neighbourhood, but could get no evidence beyond vague female gossip that one of the deceased woman's female relatives had seen a man leave her house very early in the morning, that words had passed, that the old crone who saw Lothario sneaking off had said she would tell the husband when he came home. I was at last convinced that this was about as near the truth as we were likely to get. I tried to get the case struck off the murder register, but was severely snubbed for my pains.

I have mentioned these cases because they illustrate the great need for a strong infusion of detective element into our police, a point on which, in its proper place, I shall hereafter lay much stress. In the kidnapping case the political agent had the aid of experienced native detectives from Bombay, who have always been good men—they, at any rate, elicited the truth. But in the other two cases I was helpless, I had no trained detective in the force, nor had I the funds to pay for them; I should only have been rebuked had I ventured to ask superior authority for what I needed. Similarly, I ought to have had in the old Marwari's case a man who, on some plausible pretence, would have settled down for a time in the village, and gradually ferreted out the village secrets. In this last case, also, I wanted a detective of the fisherman class to worm the truth out of the deceased's lovers and her own belongings.

CHAPTER VII.

THE MISSING TIGER; OR, CAIN AND ABEL.

I PURPOSE dealing in this chapter with the well-worn subject of unreported murders. A general and well-founded belief obtains in India that not one-half the murders committed are ever brought home to the criminal. My own experience of a lifetime has convinced me that it is hardly an exaggeration to say that not twenty-five per cent. of murders committed are even heard of.

I do not advance this startling statement from any feeling of prejudice against the Indian populations among whom I have laboured; on the contrary, the same allegation may be justly made against most European nationalities, with reference to the unlawful taking of life in all the large cities of the Old and New World. Unless I am very much mistaken, if the statistics could be compared of reported murders in Great Britain and India in any one year, it would be found that, taking due account of population, the percentage of murders reported is larger in the former than in the latter country, yet the proportion of convictions would be more numerous in Great Britain, by reason of the total want of detective agency in India.

Abandoning these speculations, however, as somewhat foreign to the subject in hand, I must point to the climate, the great distances between the stations occupied by men in authority—the magistracy and the police—and especially to the usual mode of disposing of the dead by cremation, which effectually and in a few hours after the crime destroys the principal evidence or means of tracing it.

Time was—and it is not so very long ago—when a clumsy criminal procedure, involving the dragging of witnesses from their homes for weeks and months together, led to what I may almost term the habitual combination of the people of a village in which a murder might have been committed to conceal the fact if possible. I shall make a remarkable instance of this kind the principal story of this chapter. I well remember how, in old days, it was the regular thing, first of all, for the police to assemble in force at the ill-fated village, to summon most of the villagers to the chowrié (village office) to harangue and browbeat them, to keep them for hours, and even days, from their occupations, for no other earthly reason than to display their power, and let Jack Policeman show off in office.

The case might be distant one to eighty miles from the nearest Magistrate to whom the accused and the witnesses were dragged off—the more respectable commonly refusing the niggardly maximum of four annas per diem tendered to them for their expenses; the poorer obliged by sheer poverty to accept the minimum two annas.

I must do the overworked Magistrates and Assistant-magistrates of those days the justice to say that no criminal case of any kind was ever delayed by them. It was almost a point of honour to set other duty aside, to sit down to the criminal case newly arrived, and not to leave it till it was disposed of. If it happened to be a murder case, committal being made to the sessions Judge, it had to wait till the sessions, which might be at any time—a month, two months, three months distant; there were even not a few outlying or inaccessible stations at which a full-power Judge only sat twice in a year! All the witnesses were then necessarily sent to their homes, to be collected again a few weeks or months later, and driven like a flock of sheep to the Sessions station, often a hundred or one hundred and fifty miles from their place of residence.

Conceive the intolerable annoyance, the serious loss, the risk of illness to the witnesses under such a system, and my readers will not be surprised at the desire to suppress a murder! I shall be told, "*Nous avons changé tout cela.*" So we have, to a marvellous extent. Good roads and railways, a very sufficient and a fairly efficient Magistracy, are now besprinkled over the country, but, best of all, a Criminal Sessions is held every month, even in the most benighted regions, while the power to order a special sessions is largely made use of when anything like a good case is made out for it.

It has been my lot to see much of the working of the police and criminal procedure in England since I took off my Indian harness, and I affirm that, *on the whole*, justice is much better administered in the Western Presidency than it is in England at the present moment. The remark is probably equally true for all the old presidencies, but I can only speak from my own knowledge and experience. Most people are familiar with that portion of *Truth* in which Mr. Labouchere every week pillories inefficient Magistrates, and there have been not a few cases even in the highest courts of late which have justly aroused severe criticism. I venture to affirm that the Registrar of the High Court on the Mofussil side in Bombay could not, in any one month, find in the returns of the Bombay Presidency, with its thousands of Magistrates, enough material to supply a similar number of columns for *Truth*.

After this long, but, I trust, pardonable digression, I will betake me to the tale of "The Missing Tiger." There is nothing to be alarmed at, for this is not a typical Indian "tiger story!"

Many years ago (alas, how many!), when I was engaged in the Southern Konkan upon the police duty described in the first story, I was joined in the month of October by a certain well-known lawyer. I will not give his name, but may mention that he is still alive, very flourishing in his circumstances, very portly, and *very much married*. He was anxious to see something of Mofussil tent life, to work off the heavy "tiffins," or luncheons, at the old Indian Navy Club, and to get a little shooting, for which he brought down a battery equal to anything, from a snipe to an elephant! We were making our way across to a new camp over a very rough piece of laterite country, then covered with long grass and scrub jungle. After a long forenoon after the

MEETING THE "IXPRESH."

snipe, as we struck into the main track leading to our camp, we descried a mhar (village watchman) trotting along briskly, and catching him up, I observed the man carried a letter, which, being addressed "*Urgent*" to the police havildar at my nearest post a few miles off, I took the liberty of opening and reading. It was from the police patel (head man) of a village some eight miles distant, and reported that two brothers (mhars) had gone out together in the early morning to cut grass and brushwood, when a tiger had sprung out, killed one of them, and carried off the other; that he would keep the mutilated body till sundown, and hold an inquest before burning it, and was collecting men to search for the missing man.

Now I knew the village and the neighbourhood well enough to be certain that it was most unlikely for a tiger to harbour within thirty miles of the spot. However, it was my duty to go there, and my friend of the law was very keen to try his big smooth-bore. So I sent the mhar back with a message to say the police saheb and his friend were coming as soon as possible—he, the patel, was to have as many beaters ready as he could collect—and that the police saheb would arrange about the inquest.

We went on to camp close by, whence what with breakfast, and what with my friend's complicated shooting preparations, we could not get off till after two o'clock, leaving us but two hours to cover the distance. A man on the look-out took us to a small rest-house at the side of the road, where we found the patel and a goodly crowd of beaters.

The body, stretched stark on its back on a kind of litter, was first cursorily inspected, its appearance, as it lay with arms stretched straight down the sides, appeared to bear out the report; the right side of the face was crushed and swollen, the right eye was nearly torn out, as it were, by a tiger's claw. It looked, in fact, just as if the poor wretch had received a crushing blow from behind from a tiger's paw.

I ordered it to be kept as it was, while we, beaters and all, hurried off to the scene of the tragedy, for there was not much daylight to spare. The path lay along the brink or edge of a dell, the high grass showing every track through it. The man who found the body walked first with me, and soon pointed to a depression in the dell. I made the guide and gun-bearers walk in single file, taking the lead myself, so that I could note in what direction any animal might have dragged the missing man while I sent the beaters round the hillside with my friend, with instructions to advance in a circle when I gave the signal.

This was soon done, for the scrub only extended over a small area. I then went cautiously down to the spot indicated by the guide, and there, sure enough, were abundant evidences of a severe struggle. The grass was trodden down in a circle of about eighteen feet diameter, and there was abundance of blood; *but* I instantly observed that, except by the track by which I had come down, there was no disturbance or trampling of the grass, not the faintest sign of any large beast having passed through it, or dragged anything with it!

I gave the signal for the beat to begin, however, and soon heard shouts and yells and my friend's voice in excitement, evidently running very fast. Presently as a large sounder of hog broke back through the beaters, I caught a glimpse of my poor lawyer as he came what the Yankees call "an almighty cropper" over a boulder, firing off both barrels in the fall! How the poor fellow had barked his shins! As to his gun, both barrels were dented and the stock broken! We made our way back to the rest-house, where I had torches lit and selected the jury.

At this time the patel and other villagers tried hard to persuade me just to note the appearance of the corpse as it lay, and to let them proceed to burn it; indeed, it *was* awfully "high" by that time! I insisted, however, after noting down the appearances on the front, on having it turned over on its face, and then the "murder was out!" A most ghastly sight presented itself, and the whole scene of the murder was revealed!

The poor wretch had evidently been squatting, cutting brushwood—I forgot to mention that a small bundle of it was lying in the dell covered with blood—when his brother struck him from behind with his own "koiti," or bill-hook, on the back of his head, the curved point of the implement entering his right eye. Instinctively he must have raised his left arm to ward off a second blow, for there was a deep gash and a slice of nearly-severed flesh on the under part of his arm. Several other blows, breaking the vertebræ, must then have been rained on him, till the murderer, seeing life was extinct, left him and fled.

The villagers and patel then confessed their deceit.

THE INQUEST: "MURDER WILL OUT."

[*To face p.* 80.

ANTOLOGIAS

The deceased and his brother Kannak had a long-standing feud about a miserable plot of land; probably high words passed in that fatal dell before Kannak struck his brother down. The villagers guessed the truth directly the body was found, and they had a quiet debate as to how the matter should be hushed up, none of them relishing the idea of being hurried up to the Sessions Court as I have above described.

It was the patel who suggested the "fixing up" of the body as I first saw it; the gash and flesh of the arm was plastered up somehow with cow-dung, and lying on its back the corpse looked very like a case of tiger mauling. Kannak was gone, and not likely to return! It was a long way to the police post, and the havildar might be away; if so, well and good. The "Punchayatnama," or jury's report was a simple matter, and the body could be burnt at sundown. If the policeman did turn up before, he would be easily deceived, or if not deceived, could be bribed to join in the plot and hold his tongue.

Luck was against them, however, that time. Kannak was caught in a foreign neighbouring state within a week, and duly committed for trial; he then feigned insanity, refused to eat, *et-cætera*. So the case was traversed to another Sessions that he might be watched. In due time I had the great satisfaction of giving evidence and hearing him sentenced to death. The patel afterwards got a pretty severe sentence.

There can be no doubt that but for my accidentally meeting the messenger the plot would have succeeded to the full, and the case have been recorded as one of "death by wild animals." Many and many a murder is, I am quite certain, even now reported as death from snake-bite, a false "Punchayatnama" drawn up, and the body quietly burned!

I forgot my poor legal friend; he was really seriously bruised and shaken, as well as his blunderbuss, and I doubt if he ever tried running through long grass over rocky ground again.

CHAPTER VIII.

THUGGEE.—THE MASSACRE.

It is somewhat of a coincidence that just as I was about to put together a few notes on the subject of murder by Thugs, the *British Medical Journal* should publish an article bearing materially on the subject. It is, and has been for some years, a popular belief among Indian officials that, with the suppression of the Thugs proper, who despatched their victims by strangulation, in the manner so graphically described by Captain Meadows Taylor in his 'Confessions of a Thug,' there has been a steady increase in murder by poisoning, and that those who have resorted to it are, in point of fact, Thugs, worshippers of the fell goddess Bhowáni, practising their trade, like the " Phansigars," * for the purposes of gain.

I myself doubt if there is any solid ground for this belief; my own experience has not taught me so. When I first went to India, in the early fifties, Thuggee was not quite stamped out in the older Presidencies. Duty, in connection with the tracing out of an organised system of dacoity, on several occasions took me to the Jubbulpore School of

---

* " Phansigars " take their name from " phansi," a noose.

Industry, where I have interviewed many Thugs; others have from time to time been sent down into districts I was serving in to give information, or to identify suspected Thugs. I certainly never heard from these persons that the suppression of the use of the sacred "roomal," or handkerchief, had driven the votaries of Bhowáni to the use of poison in its place; nor do I remember in official reports by the able officers, who up to the present time have superintended the suppression of Thuggee, that they were in possession of any evidence in support of the theory.

It must always be borne in mind that the discovery of murder by poisoning, whether by *dhatura*, opium, or arsenic, has year by year become easier, since the means of communication have improved. There were probably just as many, or even more, cases of poisoning before the "fifties" as since then, but they were not brought to light, because there was rarely a person competent to trace poisons in the viscera within reasonable distance of the spot where the body was found, and the very transport of the portions required for analysis was nearly impossible. Now, every native district officer knows precisely what to do. There are fairly competent medical practitioners scattered throughout the country, and it may almost be said that in most cases of suspected poisoning the viscera find their way to the Government Analyst.

I can personally vouch for Captain Meadows Taylor's having had no suspicion that Thuggee by poisoning existed when he left India, for I had the pleasure of knowing that accomplished and able officer well—I know that he believed the measures taken by Government had then led to the almost total suppression of Thuggee in every form. I can only call to mind one case of poisoning that at all resembled Thuggee, and, if I mistake not, it was subsequently proved beyond all question that the poisoners were Mahomedans from the Nizam's territory.

Not so very many years ago, during one of the many scarcities in the "arid zone" of the Western Presidency, fodder and water having already become very scarce, five Mahrattas from the south of Sholapore—which is now, I believe, a part of the Bijapore District—determined to drive over all their surplus cattle into the Nizam's territory, there to sell the beasts for what they would fetch. Their nearest route lay through a very desolate and rugged country, which forms the boundary of the British and Nizam's (or Mogulai) territories. They disposed of their herd in the course of a month, converted their money into British rupees (which attracted some attention to them), and set out on their return journey, with the cash, some fifteen hundred rupees, divided amongst them.

Being from British territory, they were unarmed, of course, and merely carried iron-shod sticks for their defence. On the borders they were overtaken by a Mahomedan, apparently of some condition, mounted on a good horse, richly caparisoned, accompanied by a man on foot, ostensibly his servant.

Both master and man were armed to the teeth, to the dismay of the Mahrattas who naturally feared that they would be attacked; but the Mahomedan "gentleman" entered urbanely into conversation, mentioned that he was in the Nizam's police service, one of a patrol recently established along the frontier to check the depredations of Hussan Khan, a noted freebooter of the day. His road, he said, for a couple of marches, was the same as theirs, and perhaps the Mahrattas had better keep with him for the time.

The simple fellows readily agreed, were regaled by their escort with any amount of boasting of his prowess, wealth, and influence, and easily induced to tell their own story, confiding to their kind escort that they carried a considerable amount of cash among them. Nothing occurred during the first night that they camped together. The two Mahomedans, of course, cooked and ate separately, but within a few paces of the Mahrattas.

Next day the march was resumed, the whole party camping as before on the bank of a small rivulet in some scrub jungle; they were to part company at daybreak, as the Mahomedans said they must go southward.

About ten the next morning another small party of herdsmen were about to encamp with their cattle at the same place, when they heard deep groans from the scrub near; proceeding to the spot they found one of the Mahrattas vomiting and writhing with pain, and apparently at the point of death. However,

THE LAST SUPPER.

[*To face p.* 86.

they attended him to the best of their power: towards evening he had revived sufficiently to tell his story, which was to the effect that he and his four companions had, one after the other, been seized with mortal sickness after their evening meal, that he believed he was the only survivor, and that the bodies of the others would be found at no great distance, probably rifled, as he found he himself had been robbed of all the money he carried.

In a few moments the bodies of his four companions were found in the bush near, lying, distorted and stiff, within a few yards of each other. Needless to say, they too had been rifled of the cash they carried.

The survivor had not much recollection of what had passed, he had not felt very well the preceding day, had therefore eaten very sparingly, and when subsequently racked by pain, he tried to crawl down to the water, and must have become insensible. Some of the food they had all eaten was found close to the camp fire, one of the good Samaritans of the second party had the sense to take possession of it, and to send two of his men back to the nearest British police post with full information. The bodies were at last taken to a dispensary some forty miles distant, where the doctor took out the viscera, bottled them, and sent them, with the food, to the Government Chemical Analyser in Bombay, who found enough arsenic to kill half a regiment.

Not a trace of the Mahomedan gentleman was ever discovered. A man was apprehended in the Mogulai territory on suspicion of being the servant, but the surviving Mahratta did not identify him. The Nizam's authorities were promptly communicated with, but their police officials were so lax that no real effort, I am sure, was ever made to trace the murderers. More than likely, the Ameens (Nizam police officers) were bribed to hush up the matter. As to our own police, they were useless over the border, and there were no detectives in the force to send to trace out the criminals at leisure.

The case caused some stir at the time, being believed by many to be a case of Thuggee poisoning. As a matter of fact, it was a simple case of poisoning for the sake of robbery, by poisoners who were genuine, and not pretended Mahomedans. There may be a few "Phansigars," or genuine Thugs, still using the holy "roomal," or handkerchief, in remote parts of native states, but I am convinced there are none left in British territory.

There are, no doubt, a tolerable number of men who poison for the sake of robbery, but even these ordinarily hail from and retreat to native states, usually administering arsenic in large quantities, because that is the easiest poison to procure, and the most rapid and certain in its effect. They have a profound belief that "dead men tell no tales."

CHAPTER IX.

CHILD-MURDER FOR ORNAMENTS.

I FEAR there is still rather a heavy annual crop of murders of children for the sake of their ornaments, but the incessant warnings of the authorities have unquestionably had some effect. Children are not allowed to run about unattended and unguarded with valuable ornaments on their bodies so much as they used to be, and I am given to understand that the record of this class of crime is steadily on the decrease.

Children, no doubt, are often merely robbed of their clothes or valuables; for among the hideous old crones who abound, especially in towns, and who live —God knows how—there are a fair number of old "Mrs. Browns," whose cupidity is often aroused by the sight of little victims like "Florence Dombey." Murder of children for the sake of their ornaments is usually the work of men, generally of the trading classes. I am afraid that I must add that the lowest classes of Marwarrees, "Goozurs," or Wanis, furnish the most instances. One remarkable case I remember, however, in which a Mahomedan, previously of the highest character and the most humane disposition, was the criminal. The story is noteworthy for other reasons, which will appear hereafter. I shall call it—

"Poor Little Saloo."

Saloo was a bright little fellow about seven years of age. His father was in charge of the ferry up an estuary not far from Bombay, plying daily from his own rather large village, by wind and tide, to the mouth of the creek. This ferryman's great crony was a Mahomedan general merchant, or large shopkeeper in the village, a man of about forty, very well to do, with a reputation for honesty, and notoriously generous and open-handed to the poor. Like most natives he was very fond of children, but, having none of his own, he always liked to see them about his shop, and petted them one and all.

He had carried Saloo about in his arms from babyhood, and the little fellow, his father being so much away from home, lived almost as much with Suliman (that was his name) as in his own house. The father almost daily brought some package or other for Suliman by the ferry-boat, thus it was an every-day occurrence for Suliman to go down to the bunder, about half a mile distant, with Saloo trotting by his side, about the time the tide served for the ferry-boat to come in. Now, the "bunder," or landing-place, was at the end of a long embankment projecting into deep water over an intervening mangrove swamp, which was only covered by a few

CALIFORNI

THE DENOUNCING BAND.

[To face p. 91.

feet of water at the very top of the tide; for the most part it was a foul and noisome stretch of deep black mud dotted with mangrove bushes.

The ferry-boat was due after dark one evening, when Suliman was seen making his way to the bunder, chatting and laughing with Saloo, who trotted by his side. When the ferry-boat at last arrived, the father hailed Suliman and asked if he had brought little Saloo. Suliman replied that he had brought him down, but that as it had got late he had sent him home again. The two friends, having made fast the ferry-boat, walked home together, accompanied by some of the passengers, and the father's being the first house they came to, he called out to "Saloo Meeya." The mother's voice replied from within that he had gone down to the bunder with "Suliman Baba." Suliman observed that he had probably gone to his shop, and that he would send the little monkey home at once.

He returned in a few minutes in the greatest agitation to report that Saloo Meeya was not there, that he was seriously afraid he had fallen into the creek. Torches were got, and all the village turned to the bunder, but the tide was at full, and no trace of the little fellow could be seen. Searching parties were down again next morning directly the tide had left the fœtid swamp uncovered, in the midst of which was soon descried a little hand and arm sticking up out of the soft mud. There was poor little Saloo, dead, with his mouth and nostrils full of mud. The little armlets encircling his arms were gone, and abrasions on the tender flesh showed that they had been wrenched off with some violence !

At the pitiful sight, Suliman, who was with the search-party, and evidently greatly agitated, screamed out that he had done it. " I was mad. Come, and I will give up the bangles." He was taken to his house, and produced the miserable trifles from a sack of rice.

I was on the spot two days afterwards, heard the wretched man tell the tale, and accompanied him to the scene of the tragedy. If ever a man felt remorse, that man felt it. He told me—and I am very sure he spoke truly—that he acted without premeditation; that he never thought of the ornaments until they were near the bunder-head, when he took Saloo up in his arms, and, in doing so, happened to feel the ornaments. "There was no one near, and 'Shaitan' took him." He carried the boy a few yards into the ooze, and, taking up a handful, crammed it into the little fellow's mouth, stifling his cries. He wrenched off the bangles, trod the little body into the mud, and, regaining the bunder-head, had time to wash his feet and hands before the ferryman's boat came up.

"Why, saheb," said he, "what did I care for? How could I want those worthless bangles? And I was so fond of Saloo Meeya, too! Not a month has passed for years that I haven't given the boy more than the worth of the bangles. I used to see them every day, and never thought of them. I was mad! It is my fate! Take me to the Judge Saheb quickly, and let me be hanged."

Hanged, of course, he was, on the very spot at which the crime was committed, for there had been overmuch of this class of crime of late; but he could not have lived long, for, without purposely abstaining from food, he could not eat, becoming at last so feeble and emaciated that he had to be carried to the scaffold. After his sentence was pronounced he asked if Saloo Meeya's father could be induced to visit him. I am glad to say the father went. The scene was, I was told, a most affecting one, the father always insisted afterwards that "Suliman Baba did not mean to do it—he was mad; it was all 'nusseeb' (fate)." And, indeed, I myself believe the man was mad, just as those ladies are mad who, without rhyme or reason, secrete things in shops. I doubt, however, if a more horrible case of kleptomania has ever occurred.

SULIMAN'S FATE.

CHAPTER X.

MURDER FROM JEALOUSY.—MURDER FROM INFIDELITY.

It is scarcely necessary to dwell at any length on those classes of crime which are neither more numerous in India than they are in England, nor peculiarly characteristic of Indians.

A month's issue of such delectable evening papers as the *Star* or *Evening News* probably record as many horrible murders by jealous husbands, wives, and lovers as are to be heard in all India in six months.

As a matter of fact, it would probably be found that in India, jealousy, whether on the part of the husband, or on the part of the lover of his mistress, is satisfied by some horrible mutilation, and stops short of taking the victim's life. Time was, and not so many years ago, that the common punishment in India for infidelity was cutting off the nose of the frail wife or paramour; in the fewer cases now recorded, the bludgeon or the knife seems to be more commonly used. There is no greater ferocity displayed in Bombay or Calcutta than in the slums of London or Paris, where most ruffians carry a knife or revolver, and use it freely, while those who do not possess a weapon find their hobnailed boots quite as efficacious. Amongst the better classes in India, such cases as we have recently read of in Europe are of the rarest occurrence, while there is no morbid eagerness or disposition to find extenuating circumstances by Judge, Juror, or Assessor.

Those—and there are many officials who ought to know better—who assert that infidelity in the conjugal relations is commoner in India, that the standard of morality is lower there than in Europe, grossly libel the people of India, especially the rural population. It is not a pleasant topic to dwell upon; but I am forced of my own knowledge and observation, and from what I have learnt from rural residents of all classes, to declare that immorality is general in most agricultural districts in England, where immoral connections are not merely tolerated, but accepted as almost a matter of course.

The very language used habitually by the women of the labouring classes in England among themselves betokens a depravity which I have never found among the "ryots." The women of an Indian family are rarely alone during the daytime, at night they usually sleep together; there are not those facilities for intrigue that exist in England, and overcrowding—promiscuous overcrowding at night, such as is common in many English cottages—is unknown.

It is when the Indian village girl, leaving her native village, joins some factory in the larger towns, or some body of labourers on a large public work, that she becomes contaminated by the abundance of temptation and opportunity.

The police have ordinarily no difficulty in tracing the perpetrators of crimes of this class; their work is cut out for them. The jealous husband rarely attempts to evade justice, or, if he tries to escape, is easily followed; there is rarely premeditation, and no preparations for escape have been made. The jealous wife usually resorts to poison, peppers the evening meal liberally with arsenic, and perhaps kills off half the unsuspecting household. The dissipated young fellow in a town, madly infatuated by some (to him) fascinating woman of the place, excited by drink or "bhang," stabs her to the death, and is caught red-handed.

The experience of most Indian police officers must be, like my own, that in ninety per cent. of the murders from jealousy, women of the town are the victims. Still, there are always instances of women murdering their husbands, or aiding in their murder by paramours.

The worst case I ever knew I will briefly relate; the actual details are too horrible for publication. I will call it—

"The Fate of Quilp."

Bhági was married to a man much older than herself, a misshapen, evil-tempered "sootar," or carpenter; very dissolute, and a drunkard, but withal a very skilful workman when sober. Sonoo strongly reminded me, in appearance, and especially in feature, of the illustrations of Quilp in Dickens' celebrated novel. Like Quilp, he would purposely absent himself from his wife; when with her, he had a fiendish delight in torturing and maltreating her generally; thus, he had branded her on various parts of her body, had cut her about here and there with his adze, and on one occasion had chopped off one of her big toes. There were, happily, no children.

Sonoo was constantly employed on public works, in and out of Bombay, as a "maistree," or foreman carpenter, and a fine young fellow called Dhondoo, a carpenter from the same village, usually worked in his gang. Bhági and Dhondoo had known each other from childhood, an illicit connection existed between them, which Sonoo had just begun to suspect, when the gang was employed in the erection of a railway station on the B. B. and C. I. Railway. Full of drink, and infuriated by jealousy, Sonoo returned to their temporary hut one evening, knocked Bhági down with a mallet and gagged her, then heating one of his smaller tools red-hot, he deliberately scored a kind of pattern on her buttock. On going to work next morning he swore that when he came back he would cut her nose off!

Bhági was not seriously injured on this occasion, but she was firmly convinced that Sonoo meant to carry out his threat. She managed to communicate with Dhondoo in the course of the day, and they determined on Sonoo's (Quilp's) fate for that evening.

Dhondoo, after sundown, secreted himself in the hut, armed with a stone-mason's hammer. Quilp, who had probably been drinking himself up to the necessary pitch, was late, and at once accosted Bhági in his usual ferocious manner. Dhondoo, stepping from his hiding-place, felled him to the ground with a blow on the back of his head. The pair then turned him round, Bhági, seating herself on his mouth and holding his hands, looked on, while Dhondoo tore the wretch's clothes from his body and kneaded him on the chest and ribs with his knees, winding up by otherwise mutilating him with the stone hammer in a manner too horrible to describe.

Quilp had probably been killed by the first blow. The lovers, waiting till all signs of life were extinct, by which time the camp was buried in sleep, carried the body to one of the numerous small "chunam" (or lime) kilns burning near, and thrust it in, head foremost. When discovered next morning, the head and shoulders were nearly consumed, but there was no difficulty in identifying Quilp's crooked legs.

I wonder if a French jury would have found "extenuating circumstances"? Dhondoo, I know, was hanged, exulting in what he had done, but Bhági got off with a long term of imprisonment.

It will be a relief to my readers, as to me, to leave the subject of murder for a time, in order to deal with forgery and perjury, the particular offences which are, if we are to believe some Indian Judges, especially rampant in India.

N.B.—This story is altogether too horrible to illustrate.

CHAPTER XI.

FORGERY AND PERJURY.

In considering these crimes it is difficult to separate forgery from its helpmeet perjury. Forgery always depends upon perjury to support and carry it to a successful issue.

Perhaps it will be convenient to deal first with perjury in its isolated form, as it presents itself to every public officer in India, from the police superintendent upwards, at every step of almost every investigation. False evidence for or against a prosecution—false evidence in support of or against a claim for money or property—false evidence, material or immaterial, to any point at issue, is to be met with and guarded against in every case; but the worst of all false evidence is that which results from what is commonly known as the "tutoring" of witnesses by the police.

I am afraid I must declare my belief that "tutoring" is commonly resorted to in India. Good cases are often broken down by being bolstered up, in what the police imagine are weak points, by false usually, unnecessary evidence. Bad cases are often supported by false evidence so cleverly concocted that the innocent are not infrequently found guilty. The motive may be excess of zeal, or, it may be, anxiety to support the known views, or even the supposed desire, of an official superior. Hundreds of such instances will occur to the mind of every Police Superintendent, Magistrate, or Judge This, the besetting sin of the Indian Police, it must be admitted, is almost unknown in England. It was increasing when I left India, it is unlikely that it will diminish till the whole Police system shall have been reformed.

Putting aside, however, perjury of this dangerous character as peculiar to India, is there any sound basis for the generally expressed official belief that other perjury is more common in India than in England?

I am one of those who, with all my Indian experience behind me, have had special opportunities in later years of studying police cases of every kind in England, of hearing what barristers and solicitors say of the civil cases in which they are concerned. The daily journals teem, too, with cases in which false swearing on one side or the other, or both, is palpable, while judges inveigh, in vain, from the bench against the prevalence of perjury. Has there ever been a worse case in India than what is known as the "Hurlbert case," to say nothing of several more recent instances of perjury in connection with will suits? Has there ever been more wholesale perjury than in the Tichborne, commonly known as the "Claimant's case"? or the Piggott part of the *Times'*

Commission, which combined forgery with false swearing?

I have been thrown in intimate contact with the English agricultural classes, and find them quite as much, if not more, addicted to lying as my old friend Bhow Patel or Bappoo Kunbi in India.

The fact is, that "service men" go out to India young, without any experience of their own countrymen; at first, from the very nature of their duties, seeing only the seamy side of native character, they become impressed with the belief that those around them have no regard for veracity—a belief so strong that a subsequent better knowledge can hardly eradicate it.

Professional men and those connected with mercantile pursuits, on the other hand, similarly ignorant of their own land, and also going out in their youth, live in large cities or stations, know nothing, or next to nothing, of the languages, and have little communication with non-English-speaking natives, and that little through the interpretation of their clerks.

Few, very few of us get to know anything of the masses of natives, their habits, their modes of thought, their inner lives. Betwixt us and them "there is a great gulf fixed," and we are apt in our self-conceit and ignorance to judge rashly, usually failing to perceive that the poor people around us have very many good qualities that should command our respect. Somehow or other it has become a settled belief that natives are habitually liars, and in the courts of law indulge the propensity with the utmost freedom. We do not know how often the native does not rightly understand his questioner; how very easily he is confused, or made to say (or misinterpreted to say) what he does not really mean.

The imperturbable Briton, though of the strictest veracity, can be and often is shown up to public scorn when in the witness-box, can be made to contradict himself and appear bent upon prevarication; *he* is being examined by his own countryman, in his own language. The native witness is often in the hands of a cross-examiner who imperfectly understands him, and has to take his evidence at second-hand. Why should we always jump to the conclusion that the native witness is bent on perjuring himself? Why not make as much allowance for the native as for the Englishman?

We come to be more charitable when we get older, and have left the East for good. We find, when it is too late, from what we see of our own countrymen and women, that we must often have judged very harshly and uncharitably in India. It is not a pleasant retrospect.

But if it is unfair exaggeration to assert that wholesale perjury is peculiarly rife in India, it is unfortunately too true that it is the land of forgers. Not that the crime prevails among, or is practised by, the people generally; it is the work of the higher castes, of the educated classes necessarily, it exactly suits the genius of the wily Brahmin.

The constant change in the *personnel* that surrounded the Peishwa's Court, the constant rise and fall among the subordinate chiefs, the constant shifting of power and influence, the "sanads" and counter "sanads" (deeds or grants) produced a chaos which it has taken many years of British rule to reduce to order. Never perhaps has Brahminical intrigue had a wider and a richer field to revel in than that afforded by the British Government, from the downfall of Bajirao to the termination of the inquiries by the hated Inam Commission. Even then a vast number of cases of titles or of claims to grants of land or money remained unsettled, while others were allowed to be reopened on grounds more or less well founded. It would be highly interesting to know how many palpably forged documents, how many tainted deeds, were produced before the various tribunals between 1820 and 1860.

Then or about that time came a flood of legislation connected with suits for money and various changes in the stamp laws, which have yielded an abundant harvest to a class of men ever on the watch for their opportunity. One of the ablest Judges once assured me that every change in the law with reference to limitation of suits, to stamps, or even to registration, produces a "flush of forgery" throughout the Presidency. How far that may be true, whether it be an exaggeration, I leave judicial experts to determine.

The police are not usually called upon to act in cases of perjury or forgery, except when these crimes crop up in the course of the investigation of a conspiracy for some other nefarious purpose. The perjurer is, or can be, committed for trial by the Court before which the offence is discovered. The forgery is commonly brought to light in a court of justice or before some tribunal, which impounds the suspected document, and refers the case to the magistrate.

I remember, however, one notable case in which the police under me were employed with considerable success in unearthing an organised gang of forging swindlers. If my memory serves me right, it was somewhere about 1860 or 1861 when an Act was passed, the effect of which was to prevent the filing of suits for the recovery of money on unstamped bonds after a certain date. The same sort of thing must have occurred all over the country, but, to the best of my belief, no formal inquiry was instituted elsewhere.

The Judge of the district in which I was then serving—who was conspicuous for his remarkable knowledge of the vernacular and his intimate acquaintance with native life and character—was struck, first of all, by the enormous number of suits filed on unstamped bonds for petty sums in a particular subdivision of his jurisdiction. He next noticed, as they came up before him in shoals on appeal, that for some time it was invariably the defendant who appealed against the decree of the Lower Court, and that all he could allege in the face of an apparently clear case against him was, that the bond was a forgery and that he was not indebted.

Very soon, however, he observed that the appellant

was usually the original plaintiff, who, having been non-suited because of the defendant proving repayment or producing and proving a receipt, alleged that the receipt was a forgery.

Quietly analysing the cases for a few months he found that in all such cases the plaintiff was one of some eighteen money-lenders; that the same vakils were always employed in the Court below; that latterly the defendants were always represented by two well-known rival vakils in the same Court!

The Judge thereupon represented the facts and his suspicions confidentially to the magistrate, and in due course I was instructed to take the matter up. It was no easy matter to decide how to act, for I had no clue but the Judge's suspicions. After some weeks, however, I learnt enough through the hangers-on to the particular sub-judge's court (Moonsiff he was called in those days) to convince me that one of the eighteen plaintiffs was at the head of the conspiracy, so I took my chance of finding something useful in searching his house. It was not a very irregular proceeding, but we *had* sometimes to be irregular in those days.

The result was beyond my expectations. The police found a "roomal," or bundle, not even hidden away, in which there was a kind of rough diary and a list of persons who had been, or were to be, victimised, with a few details as to their means and ability to pay, and their deceased fathers' names and dates of death, if the son was to be sued on his father's bond. There were plenty of letters from the partners in the fraud, and a few from the vakils they employed, sufficiently incriminating them. Indeed, there was no attempt at concealment. Some of the letters discussed what should be done now that the two other vakils had hit upon the dodge of putting in forged receipts, or of proving payment by " good " witnesses. Lastly, there was a good supply of spare paper bearing the signs of age.

The matter then passed out of my hands, and the Judge came down on circuit and held a departmental inquiry. I left the district about that time, but afterwards heard that the four vakils had their " sanads " (or licences to practise) cancelled, and that the Moonsiff, an incapable old fool, was compulsorily retired. No doubt some of the " eighteen " were prosecuted, but with what result I do not know.

It came out that these eighteen villains, residing in different villages in the jurisdiction, used to meet periodically—" in committee," as it were—with a list of the persons whom they thought " good " for small amounts of ten, twenty, or fifty rupees. Other necessary particulars having been collected, the committee then decided who should be next sued, and for what amount; who of the eighteen should be the nominal plaintiff; who should write the bond, and who should witness it. Suitable paper was selected, and the bond was then drawn up. The signature of the victim was a simple matter enough, for he was invariably illiterate, and a ploughshare or some such symbol served as his mark. In Court the wretched victim was confronted by the evidence of the nominal lender, of the man who wrote the bonds, and of the two witnesses to the payment and to his signature. He had no defence. The bond was often dated several years back, and it was useless for him to contend that it was a forgery.

The other vakils in the court, of course, soon scented the fraud, and two of them hit upon the expedient of proving payment in some cases by a receipt, written by some enemy of the "eighteen," in which the nominal plaintiff's signature was boldly

THE FORGERS' STOCK-IN-TRADE.

forged, and by the evidence of two false witnesses to the repayment; but in the majority of cases it was found sufficient to produce witnesses only. And so the game of "tit-for-tat" went merrily on, to the great contentment of the vakils, till the occupation of the wily eighteen was nearly gone, and the astute Judge blew up the conspiracy.

On another occasion my police, in searching the house of a young Brahmin for stolen jewellery, came across what must have been the stock-in-trade of his deceased father, a very notorious old rascal in his time, viz. three copper dies (fabricated, of course) of the seals of certain neighbouring chiefs, several blank sheets of venerable-looking native paper, and a small book, in which the amiable old gentleman had evidently been practising various handwritings and signatures.

Not very long before I left the country, a complete set of false merchants' account-books extending over five years fell into my hands, but, that is another story, which will be found in its proper place later on.

CHAPTER XII.

DACOITY.

WHEN I first became connected with the police, dacoity still existed nearly as it is depicted in 'Pandoorang Hurree'* and the stirring tales by Meadows Taylor. Sprinkled liberally about the country were well-known dacoit leaders, counting adherents in every village, or at least informants, among all but the highest castes. At every "Dusserah" festival in the month of October, in imitation of the practice of all great Maratha leaders, each band assembled secretly by night, at the summons of its acknowledged chief, in some deserted fort or temple, to settle a general programme of proceedings for the coming season's campaign; the names of the selected victims; the kind of booty expected; the probability of resistance, or of interference by the authorities (then held in no small contempt); modes of communication; of disposing of the booty; in short, every detail of the operations to be undertaken was solemnly discussed and decided.

New members were then admitted, and sworn to

* Re-edited by Sir Bartle Frere.

fidelity on the "kuttar," or dagger, or some other weapon or emblem; after the sacrifice of a fowl or a goat, usually to "Bhowanee," but frequently to some other patron deity, the band separated before cock-crow, and then began the season's dacoities, and a lively time for the police everywhere till the approach of the monsoon (annual rains), when the band reassembled, dividing the spoil, to repair each man to "winter quarters" in his own village.

The monsoon months were mostly given up to revelry and debauchery, but were also utilised for gathering information for the next "Dusserah" meeting.

The lower classes, the out-castes, did not drink habitually then as they do now, so the "Dusserah" meeting was a very solemn business, at which the strictest sobriety prevailed. Connected with every band were at least two "Gosais," "Bawas," "Faquirs," or other religious mendicants, who acted partly as their jackals, partly as their messengers, partly as their informants to give warning of the movements of the authorities, or of treachery within the ranks of the band itself. The author of 'Pandoorang Hurree' has admirably depicted these incarnate fiends in the ubiquitous and powerful "Gosai," who is one of the chief characters in the book.

There was usually a "sonar," or goldsmith, among the gang, by whom ornaments were soon melted down, and he was, generally speaking, quite honest towards his comrades; silken and other cloths were safely deposited with some friendly shopkeeper, but in the end usually found their way fragmentarily to the many mistresses of the band.

"Receivers," in the ordinary police acceptation of the word, there were none, and "honour among thieves" was almost religiously observed. Many "patels," or headmen, were, of course, friendly, and the gang had many harbours of refuge, numerous strongholds to retreat to in rough country; while individual robbers, if closely pursued, could always count on finding some friendly succour at hand, or on being, if not concealed, at least passed on to friendly hands, while pursuers were delayed or put on a false scent. Women idolised them for their lavishness, sympathised with them, gloried in their adventures, and acted as their scouts everywhere: all the odds were in favour of the fugitive and against the police.

Nevertheless, as the country settled down, the persistent and devoted zeal of the picked officers in the police (*they were picked in those days*), their untiring and ceaseless pursuit of dacoit leaders, and, above all, the generally strict enforcement of responsibility of villages under a well-known section of the Elphinstone Code, were gradually driving dacoit bands over British boundaries into Native States, when the wave of the great Mutiny swept down upon us, and immediately an epidemic of dacoity raged throughout the Western Presidency. The Bheel rising in Khandeish and Ahmednugger, the disquietude among the Kolis along the Ghauts, and the open rebellion of the Waghiris in the north put the country in a ferment, every freebooter in Native States, especially along the long line of the "Moglai" (Nizam's Dominions), took courage, and resumed operations over the border with renewed ardour.

I remember in my own small charge there were no fewer than twenty-two dacoities in a single month. How order was at length restored, and at what cost of valuable lives to Government, must still be fresh in the minds of many yet serving in the Bombay Presidency.

One remarkable feature in the dacoities of those three or four troublous years was, however, that the ancient organisation of dacoity as above described was to a great extent destroyed, and, as I believe, survives now only in Central India and the worst governed Native States.

Every now and again, it is true, some Honia, or Tantia, or Hussan Khan bursts like a comet on the country, gathering to him a few reckless wretches. He succeeds in disturbing the country, and for a while leads the police an awful dance; but there is no strong tie between him and his followers, no such freemasonry and brotherhood, no such mutual confidence, as subsisted among the organised professionals of days gone by.

There is no honour among *these* thieves; they commonly betray each other, what booty they secure is no longer safe in the hands of any member of the band, to be honestly divided at some subsequent time, but is hastily shared, and disposed of at a fraction of its value to petty dealers and shopkeepers, and even to wily Brahmins in the neighbourhood. Nay, more, it is a matter of common notoriety that these last-named immaculate gentlemen have of late years (to use a slang phrase) "put up" many of the dacoities and burglaries that have been committed by half-starved Kolis, Bheels, and the like, first of all working on their fears, exciting their cupidity, suggesting the victims, supplying information regarding them, and then, the robbery completed, appropriating the proceeds; afterwards, without the smallest compunction, if it suited their purpose, or to secure their own safety, indirectly betraying them into the hands of the police.

Does any one now doubt that the great dacoity at Panwell at a wedding feast was "put up" by Brahmins? or that all the poor devils of Kolis and others who were shot, or hanged, or transported during the so-called "Wasoodeo Bulwant Phadki Rebellion" some ten years ago were simple tools in the hands of Brahminical "Fagins"? These men were well known to, but could not be reached by, the police. Unless they are shamefully libelled, they continue to play the same game wherever opportunity offers up to the present day.

The halo of romance, such as it was, has been lifted from dacoity—one crime may be more daring, more brutal, more successful than another, and that is all; otherwise, the history of one dacoity of the present day is very much the history of all dacoities that occur, and a very dreary, commonplace history it is. I do not call to mind one case that

I

merits special notice for many years past, or that was not fully reported at the time in all the newspapers, but I remember a terrible instance of dacoit revenge, which will not be out of place in this chapter.

Before relating it I should like to add a few words in general commendation of the method adopted of late years by the Government in dealing with any recrudescence of dacoity on the appearance of men like Honia, Tantia, and many others whom it is unnecessary to mention. Nothing connected with police administration has more impressed the native mind, nothing has tended so much to repress this kind of crime, than the relentless, dogged manner with which known leaders have been hunted down through weeks and months and years.

But there is often too much deliberation, and a reluctance to sanction the only plan that will succeed; there is also a niggardliness in the matter of rewards. A very few weeks suffice to show whether the ordinary police staff of a district is equal to the often incessant and harassing labour of hunting down a gang of freebooters, and, above all, of securing the leader. This point being clear, no time should be lost in deputing to the district a special officer selected from among the numerous young officers who have shown aptitude for such service. He goes down to assist, not to supersede, the District Superintendent; he goes literally to hunt down the gang, or the man, by untiring pursuit, having at his disposal sufficient picked men, relying upon the hearty co-operation of the local police.

No District Superintendent I have ever heard of who was worth his salt has felt himself aggrieved in such a case—many of their own accord have asked for such assistance. The ordinary duties of an active Superintendent are much heavier than the public is aware of, therefore he absolutely needs extra assistance to cope with outbursts of crime of this character.

Then as to rewards; Government are given, or used to be given, to haggling over the amount to be offered. District Superintendents refrain from asking for enough, the Magistrate perhaps cuts that down, and Government "economise" still further, forgetful that an outlaw in the flush of his success is able to, and often does, outbid them in the quarters from which information may be obtained. Rewards are not very fruitful of results at any time, but to offer an inadequate reward is worse than useless, because it only brings ridicule on Government.

The energy, activity, and zeal of district police officers have done much to stamp out dacoity in the Western Presidency. A little more promptitude and generosity on the part of Government itself will work wonders, though the crime will always crop up now and again when circumstances favour it, and reckless men exist to take advantage of them.

A Dacoit's Revenge.

There must still be a few officers in Western India who remember the outbreak of the Bheels in October 1858, and how Bhagoji Naique (whose career I hope soon to recount) opened the ball by shooting Captain Henry, the Superintendent of the Ahmednugger Police, in an affray near Sinnur; how, with comparatively few exceptions, the majority

YESOO BHEEL.

of the Bheels abandoned their villages and took to dacoity under Bhagoji and sundry of his lieutenants.

At this time there was living in a village, on an important cross road in that neighbourhood, an old Bheel named Yesoo, a personal friend of Bhagoji. His village was a favourite camping-place for European officers on tour, by reason of a fine "tope" (grove) of mango trees, and the existence of good quail and hare shooting in the vicinity. Yesoo saw much of them, both in the field and in his capacity of head watchman; he was a good old fellow all round, withal very amusing, and he had an evident predilection for Sahebs generally.

Yesoo, hearing that Bhagoji had determined to " go out," as it was termed—that is to say, to encamp in the jungles with all the followers he could collect— went to see him, and tried to dissuade him from so fatal a step. After Henry's death Yesoo refused to join the rebels, and in view of his age and a slight lameness, he was excused by them and left in peace, they never suspecting for a moment that he had completely thrown in his lot with the Sahebs, and was already secretly supplying the Magistrate with very valuable information as to the origin and progress of the outbreak.

His story was, that about six months before, an emissary of Nana Saheb, or of his notorious lieutenant, Tantia Topee, made his appearance in the neighbourhood—there were plenty of such emissaries about then, as we subsequently learned—that a meeting took place at or near the town of Sungumnair, between this emissary, a wealthy Purdèsi residing in the town, Bhagoji, the chief Bheel Naique, and Jimma Naique, the head of the Koli tribe along the Syhadri range of mountains; that it was arranged that immediately after the rains Bhagoji was to lead off with the Bheels; Jimma was to follow suit with the Kolis; and when the country was thoroughly disturbed and ripe for it, Tantia Topee was to force his way southward through Khandeish with a well-equipped army and overrun the Deccan. The Purdèsi gentleman was to act as local agent and keep Tantia informed of the progress of events.

This story was otherwise corroborated (if I remember rightly) by intercepted correspondence. Bhagoji, true to his word, accordingly "led off" with his Bheels, and Jimma, no doubt, would have fulfilled his promise with the Kolis, but Government stepped in and raised a Koli corps on good pay all round—Jimma being made native commandant on large allowances—their duty being to pursue and capture Bhagoji!

It was far too good a thing for the Kolis to throw over. Of course, Jimma and Bhagoji had a perfect understanding, it was remarkable how unfortunate the Kolis were in always being *just* too late to catch the Bheels. Many a wild-goose chase was your humble servant led in vain pursuit of the nimble Bhagoji.

Tantia Topee, as all the world knows, *did* make his attempt to break into Khandeish, and was within an ace of succeeding. The Purdèsi, I fancy, soon discovered that the climate of Sungumnair would not long agree with him, for he disappeared on the first opportunity.

But to return to my story. One of Bhagoji's most trusty adherents in the early part of the so-called rebellion was one Hanmant, a young Bheel of some influence in and around the neighbourhood of Yesoo's village. No reliable evidence of his having been in any of the subsequent fights with our troops, or of his having taken part in any particular dacoity, was on record, but he certainly led strong bodies of Bheels for Bhagoji, and in short he was very much wanted by the police. Subsequently, when Bhagoji's star was on the wane, and the amnesty was proclaimed, Hanmant returned and settled quietly down in his own village.

Yesoo, by this time, was well known to have been a Government informer, and indeed gloried in it. This, seemingly, did not affect Hanmant much; he attempted to renew the most friendly relations with Yesoo, would go over to see and chat pleasantly with the old fellow, tried to persuade him to bring his family over to his (Hanmant's) own village, with a view to a little shooting. But Yesoo was a wary old fellow, and kept the young man, as much as he could, at arm's length. Finding all attempts to conciliate old Yesoo, or to get him away from his village (where he was comparatively safe with his two sons and other Bheels in the Bheelwarra, or Bheel quarter) to be unavailing, Hanmant conceived and carried out the following diabolical plot.

Taking some fifteen or twenty of his own people, and a few more Bheels who had sworn to be revenged on Yesoo, he repaired one night to Yesoo's village, silently surrounded the Bheel quarter, and then sent one of his men to fire the village stackyard at the other side of the village. Just as he anticipated, the alarm was no sooner given than every male Bheel in the "Warra,"* including Yesoo and his two sons, went off at best speed to the fire, the women and children collecting outside their huts to view the blaze. In an instant the revengeful gang surrounded the "Warra," and with his own hand Hanmant cut down and horribly mutilated Yesoo's two wives and daughters, the other women were gagged and bound, and then Hanmant and a select few, armed with matchlocks, lay in ambush by the path Yesoo and his sons must return by.

Yesoo he shot with the muzzle nearly touching his body, and the sons and one Bheel who showed fight were disposed of by his comrades; the other Bheels dispersed while Hanmant and his gang quietly returned home.

Suspicion, of course, fell immediately upon Hanmant. One of his confederates peached. Hanmant escaped into the jungle, but was caught half-famished about a week afterwards. Ultimately he and two accomplices were executed at the scene of the murder, Hanmant exulting up to the last moment in the dreadful deed, which he had been brooding over for nearly five years. What a "study of revenge!"

* Bheels always live outside the village proper.

THE BHEEL'S REVENGE.

[To face p. 120.

UNIV. OF
CALIFORNIA

CHAPTER XIII.

WRECKING.

WHEN piracy was finally put down on the Malabar Coast—which by the way was not so very long ago*—the various castes of seafaring men, the fishermen, the Kolis, the Bhandaris, and others, naturally took to wrecking in various ways. If native tradition is to be relied upon, the favourite plan of operations was somewhat as follows up to quite as late as 1850.

When the coast opened after the monsoon a confederate crew, to the number of fifteen or twenty, would collect together and repair to Surat or Bombay, or some other considerable port, where the larger native craft were laid up for the monsoon, for the purpose of engaging with a native shipowner to work a vessel for the season up or down the coast, as the case might be. A handsome sum was demanded, and usually paid down in cash, by way of advance to the crew. They elected their own "Tindal" or "Serang" (captain) from among themselves.

Messing and living together on board, they took

* The good ship *Ranger* was pirated and towed into Viziadroog in September 1812. *Vide* Grant Duff's 'History of the Mahrattas.'

no one into their confidence; they wanted no confederate on shore, they could consult with perfect safety at sea; then they waited with the utmost patience till the time came when, with a valuable cargo on board, they were sufficiently near the spot previously selected (which was always near the homes of some of them), and taking advantage of any squally weather that would be excuse enough, they would deliberately run the craft ashore at night, previously providing for their own safety in the "puggar," or jolly-boat, in which they would land just about the time the vessel struck, and pretend that they had been wrecked in her.

There were no inconvenient telegraphs and no postal service, to speak of, in those piping times; nor were there prying Police or Magisterial authorities anywhere, except at large ports.

The little game was thoroughly understood and enjoyed by the villagers in the vicinity of the wreck, who crowded down "to help" in "saving" the cargo. It was an understood thing that all shared who worked, after the crew were satisfied. There were always wily "Goozar," or Brahmin or Khojah traders attracted to the spot, who would buy anything *at a price*, from a bag of "copra" (cocoanut kernels) to a bale of silk; and the whole cargo, whatever it was, was dispersed among the villages and along the neighbouring creeks weeks before the serang (captain) and two or three of the crew found their way to the owners at Bombay, Surat, or elsewhere, and reported that the good ship *Durria Dowlat* had sprung a leak and foundered at sea, or had been driven ashore in a gale, or met with some other disaster, resulting in a total loss.

Wonderfully graphic would be the serang's description of the catastrophe, how he and all hands did their utmost to save the "dear old ship," what perils they encountered, what sufferings they underwent—in fact, how they were the most faithful and courageous of servants, to whom a large instalment of compensatory "bakshish" was obviously due, with the promise of another ship next season!

The busy, prosperous, good-natured "shettia," or merchant, listened with staring gaze and open mouth, almost always swallowing the whole story, commiserated the wretched sailors, and bountifully remunerated them. He had, perhaps, fifty large native craft, or more, plying up and down the coast. His "nasib" (luck) had been bad on this occasion, no doubt, but he must expect to lose a vessel now and again. His other ventures, however, had been fairly successful, and his profit and loss account, after all, would not look so bad at next Diwali!*

If haply he harboured any suspicion of foul play, what *could* he do? The *Durria Dowlat* had been lost perhaps two or three months before, and on a part of the coast to which he was an utter stranger. It was a long and tedious and, probably in those

---

* The festival of Diwali occurs on 26th October, when all traders close the year's accounts, pray to them, and illuminate the house-front regardless of expense. Hence the name : "dipa," a lamp, and "awali," a vow.

days, a dangerous land journey. He would have to lay out no end of money to induce the authorities to exert themselves in inquiry. He could not afford to leave his thriving business on what in all probability would turn out to be a wild-goose chase; so he shrugged his jolly fat shoulders, perhaps made a mental note not to employ that serang again, if he could help it, held his tongue, and wrote the *Durria Dowlat* off as lost at sea.

The serang and his merry men, on the other hand, took very good care from the outset not to lay themselves open to suspicion. In all probability they worked splendidly in getting the "Shibad" (large native vessel) ready for sea; they made perhaps three successful voyages in her, usually reserving their grand *coup* for the last trip before the monsoon, when the weather is apt to be unsettled. The little affair over, they were not such fools as to ship together again for two or three years, if ever; and, indeed, they usually made so large a haul that they could afford to lie by as simple fishermen for a season or so, trading in a small way on their own account for a time.

When it is remembered that in those days there were no British India or other company's steamers calling regularly for cargo at every port along the coast, that for every native craft now plying there were then a hundred, it can be readily understood what a splendid field of operations was open to these dacoits of the deep till quite the middle of the century, when communications of all sorts had improved, the country had settled down, and law and authority were beginning to be enforced.

Much of my own information was picked up from old nacodas and serangs (captains and commanders). One of them, in particular, was in 1863 a very prosperous timber merchant, whose father I shrewdly suspect to have been one of the most successful operators along the seaboard. I make no doubt his son piously aided him in his younger days. The father began life as a common khalassee (seaman), left his son five of the largest native craft ever built, and a thriving trade, which ultimately required thirty-one huge vessels, carrying teak from the southern ports. His cunning old eyes glistened and his mouth appeared to water as he told of richly-laden "dhows" and "buttelas"* run ashore under many a headland I wot of.

"There was no real danger; there was no risk in it, saheb!" he used to say; "no one cared for the Sirkar then, and there are so many soft spots on which to beach a vessel when one knows the coast." And, indeed, I could quite believe him on the last point, for it is not so very many years ago that I was engaged in an inquiry into the loss of a large Arab vessel, which tacked off and on along a sandy reach near "the wooded slopes of Barondi," and was then deliberately beached while a few horses on board landed or rather made to swim ashore. If that ship was not intentionally lost for the sake of the insurance money I am very much mistaken. At any rate,

* Native ships of the larger sorts.

the insurance was claimed, and had to be paid after some demur by the native underwriters.

Since 1850, perhaps, sea dacoity, as I must call it, has developed a milder type. Vessels cannot be intentionally beached and their cargoes got rid of without the owners receiving the news in a few days; but native craft are, as I believe, often run ashore or deliberately scuttled after having been insured for four or five times their value. After all, the native owners are only taking a leaf out of the white man's book. Audacious frauds of this kind have not unfrequently come before the public in England; Mr. Plimsoll proved a few years ago that many ships had been sent to sea known to be unseaworthy, ill-found, and under-manned, with the intention that they should founder or be lost in the first heavy weather. And was not a splendid ship deliberately scuttled as she was leaving Bombay harbour some twenty years ago?

We are not so immaculate that we can presume to cast stones at our Aryan brother in respect of sins like these; nor, again, may we inveigh against the hideous practice that formerly prevailed at certain points of the seaboard of luring vessels on to the rocks by means of lights dexterously shown on shore in dark nights. If it be true that many a boat and ship has thus been wrecked on the Malabar Coast, and especially in the vicinity of Angria's Colaba, it is no less true that the Cornish coast had an even more evil reputation. In neither country is this barbarous crime now heard of.

So, again, the pillaging of craft accidentally

ANGRIA'S COLÁBA.   [*To face p.* 126.

UNIV. OF
CALIFORNI

stranded, the robbing of the corpses cast up by the ocean, is now the exception and not the rule, as it was in years gone by. When a tempest sweeps the coast and drives hundreds of pattimars * ashore, the people turn out to help and save, not to "loot" and murder, as they habitually did in the good old times.

There is a file on the old records of the South Konkan—if it has not shared the fate of many valuable documents torn up or burnt to make room for the comparatively worthless official correspondence of late years. In that file was the history of the general looting for miles along the coast in the vicinity of the "Washisti" river, after perhaps the most awful cyclone of the present century. Barrow Ellis—whose name is even yet familiar as a household word in that region—was then Assistant Collector, he passed weeks on the spot, tracing out stolen cargo, recovering ornaments and valuables torn from hundreds of bodies cast up by the waves. For days together the entire population along the shore, from "twice born" Brahmins downwards, had been quarrelling over their plunder, leaving the corpses of the drowned, of both sexes, stripped, naked, unburied, unburnt, to be dragged about the beach by packs of village dogs and jackals. A ghastlier tale was never told. The far-reaching inquiries instituted by Barrow Ellis, resulting as they did in the severe punishment of some hundred of the offenders—many of them persons of high caste and good position—

* Smaller craft.

no doubt produced a lasting and salutary effect all along the coast.

A case, however, occurred within my own official experience not many years ago, which is worth relating, because of the success which attended the attempt to enforce village responsibility for crime committed within the village limits.

That year the monsoon burst unusually early, about the middle of May. I was a long distance away from the district headquarters, making my final inspection of police posts before the rains set in. It did not surprise me to learn that several belated pattimars (native craft), working their way on their last trip of the season up to Bombay, had been driven ashore.

Among others a large "buttela," laden with casks of cocoanut oil from Cochin, was reported to have run on a sandbank at the entrance of a creek to which she was making for shelter from the gale. The village patel, or foujdar, stated apparently full particulars.

"There was no loss of life. The crew, some eighteen or twenty Cutchee sailors, had easily got ashore when the tide receded, but the vessel, it was said, had since rolled over on her side, and her cargo of oil barrels had all been washed out of her and carried out to sea; if any were recovered they would be taken proper care of, and the 'Sirkar' duly informed, but the sea ran so high, it was feared there would be no salvage. The Cutchee crew would not wait for any inquiry, but had started at once overland to report the loss to their employers. No one understood their language, but, so far as could be made out, they had sufficient money for their expenses in their waist-belts, and as they were a rough 'zabberdasti' lot of men, no attempt had

THE WRECK AT TALEKERI.

[To face p. 123.

been made to detain them, nor were their names or the names of the Bombay owners known. The buttela itself, except in so far as it was embedded in the sand, had broken up, and there was no wreckage worth taking possession of."

The report, in short, read satisfactorily enough, beyond that it was unusually long-winded for a village report, it was sufficiently plausible. It had been sent to the Native Magistrate of the sub-district, a respectable old fossil, who naturally did not trouble himself to make any inquiry on the spot, and who simply forwarded it for information, expressing his opinion that there was nothing to be done, and that the foujdar and villagers of Talekeri had done their best under the circumstances.

However, it seemed advisable to ascertain what the name, tonnage, and value of the buttela's freight were. I accordingly addressed an official letter to the Commissioner of Police in Bombay, requesting him to institute inquiry in the bazaar, and to find out if the crew had arrived safely at their journey's end, and if they had reported the loss of their ship. Meantime, I then repaired to headquarters for the monsoon, where my friend Colt, of whom I have made mention in former papers, had already arrived.

A week or two had elapsed when Colt one morning drew my attention to an ambiguously-worded letter from a correspondent in the local vernacular paper. It was headed "Rumoured Wrecking at Talekeri; how our admirable new police are humbugged," or words to that effect; and it went on to state that the richly-laden buttela, wrecked in May, had been

K

gutted by the villagers, who, if all that was said were true, had appropriated hundreds of barrels of oil, besides bales of spices, after driving off the wretched crew of foreigners. "Cocoanut oil, needless to say, is cheap just now along the Talekeri creek," was the conclusion.

For some time the detectives we naturally sent down at once were completely baffled in their attempts to obtain any tangible proof of the newspaper's allegations. The villagers of Talekeri and the boatmen on the creek stuck to each other and would not peach. The Bombay police had not been able to find any of the Cutchee crew, who, it seemed, having really reported the wreck to their owners had left at once for their native country, Cutch, in which, in those days, finding a "wanted" man was as difficult as the proverbial looking for a needle in a bundle of hay.

The anonymous newspaper correspondent continued to deride us, and we were at our wits' end with rage, convinced that the story was mainly true, but unable to lay our hands on any clue. By the merest luck it appeared at last. An ordinary theft occurred in Talekeri itself, and in searching the house of a suspected person the police found traces of the earth floor of an out-house having been disturbed, dug it up, and, lo and behold, two casks of oil were unearthed! In the excitement that followed, while the house-owner was being arrested, his old mother "gave tongue" freely, indignantly protesting that if her poor son was to be "run in" about the buttela's oil, the police had best put the whole village into chowkey, from the foujdar or patel downwards, for they were all in it!

Most of the houses and huts in Talekeri and adjacent villages were then searched; though little was found in them, the people still remaining staunch to each other, the detectives got a hint that it would be worth while exploring along the sand dunes that fringed the beach, and, sure enough, at various spots some forty or fifty casks, the spars and sails of the buttela, and the great copper "handi," or cooking-vessel of the crew, were found buried in the sand.

The man originally apprehended then made a clean breast of it, implicating at least half the village, besides many fishermen and Kolis of neighbouring villages also. He was brought up to headquarters for safety, his trial being held over while the facts discovered were brought to the notice of the Government, which put pressure on the Cutch Durbar, through the Resident, so that before the fair season opened the Nacoda and three of the crew were found and their evidence taken in support of the newspaper story. It was then clear enough that a very serious outrage had occurred, and that although, of course, Brahmins, Wanis, and petty shopkeepers had not taken any active part in gutting the buttela, they had connived at its being gutted by Kolis and fishermen, had acted as receivers in buying and disposing of the stolen cargo, and had, in fact, reaped more profit from the crime than the actual wreckers.

Our District Magistrate had served a great deal in Guzerat, where, under the old Elphinstonian Code, he had seen the responsibility of villages constantly brought home to villages in cases of highway robbery, dacoity, and the like, when the robbers, or the property stolen, had been traced to the village walls. It went very much against his grain to let the people of Talekeri go scot-free: he would not be content with the conviction of the one man in custody, who was probably not half so deserving of punishment as scores of his neighbours in higher position.

He therefore directed that proceedings should be instituted against the whole village under the particular section I have before alluded to, which had been incorporated in the Criminal Procedure Code, then newly become law. A notice under his signature was accordingly affixed to the village temples and mosques, proclaiming that the trial would take place at the village on a certain day in November; and I was instructed to arrange with the Police Commissioner in Bombay that the three Cutchee sailors and an interpreter should be sent down to headquarters in time, so that I should take them and the man in custody down with me to Talekeri, to there conduct the prosecution in person. Colt was notoriously prejudiced against the villagers, so another Assistant Magistrate was told off to try the case.

He pitched his camp in a cocoanut plantation on the seaside, with the aid of an extra escort I had supplied him with, got the reluctant villagers assembled, read the notice or proclamation under the Criminal Procedure Code section in point, and the charge, and adjourned proceedings till the following day, so that the villagers might select and nominate a "Panch," or committee, to represent them in defence.

I had not yet arrived, and the villagers not knowing what evidence, or, indeed, that any evidence had been secured, except the confession of the man in custody, were decidedly defiant and insolent in their demeanour to the Assistant Magistrate, openly laughing the idea to scorn of anything coming of the proceedings under a section they had never heard of before, much less seen in operation.

I arrived, however, by boat with my witnesses in the course of the night, but purposely refrained from landing till the Assistant Magistrate had well commenced proceedings, which he did by recording the names of the committee of defence and a kind of plea of not guilty.

My appearance with the Cutchees had the effect of a thunderbolt on the assemblage, which was enhanced by the Nacoda running up and identifying some of the Panch (committee) as having been some of those present when the looting took place, to whom he had appealed in vain for protection.

To be brief: the prosecution carried all before it. There was practically no defence; *suave qui peut* was the line adopted by the committee, each caste denying its complicity and accusing the other castes. The estimated value of the cargo, some five thousand rupees, was then ordered to be levied as a revenue demand from the villagers, but within forty-eight hours the head people of the village somehow made up the amount. There the matter ended, for no attempt whatever was made to appeal. I suppose the people were so divided by dissensions that they could not agree on the basis for appeal. Of course, the fine was in due course paid over to the owners of the buttela in Bombay. As to the fellow in whose house the first casks were found, he was let off with a nominal punishment. I fancy the fine was a very small part of the penalty suffered by the villagers. Endless quarrels and dissensions arose among them, and for many months the vernacular papers held Talekeri up to public ridicule, while every time a European officer passed through the place he always asked the price of cocoanut oil!

CHAPTER XIV.

HOUSEBREAKING.

If dacoity is becoming easier to follow up, or gradually diminishing, housebreaking, on the other hand, is, or was lately, on the increase, and more often than not baffles the Police entirely.

It is not that the organisation of professional burglars has improved of late years, or that they are more expert than they were, say five-and-twenty years ago; on the contrary, they no longer work in large armed and dangerous gangs as they used to do. Very rarely do they display any marked skill or ingenuity such as we formerly heard of, when tunnels were not unfrequently made from without under the foundations of the jail-like buildings in which prosperous bankers resided.

I can call to mind one instance of the kind. It was in one of those walled villages so common in the Deccan. A large bridge was under construction by the Public Works Department over a stream just outside the village, and a number of quarrymen and charcoal-burners settled down in huts outside the walls while the work proceeded; the muccadums or foremen of the gangs found lodging in the village itself, where resided but one man of means, a prosperous Patel, also the village sowcar or banker, reputed always to keep a considerable sum in cash, and ornaments of great value, in a treasury chamber within his dwelling.

The house was very substantially built of coarse rubble about ten feet above a solid plinth, the only entrance being by a heavy teak doorway with iron-spiked bosses all over it, secured from within by strong bars or bolts. A half-door, as massive as the gate itself, and as well secured, was let into it, and ordinarily sufficed for the ingress and egress of the residents, the main gate being only opened morning and evening for the passage of the cattle into a spacious courtyard, around which they were tethered at night in the open verandah along two sides of the square. The third side of the square facing the gateway was built in up to the edge of the verandah, and divided into living chambers. On the left hand of the gateway, similarly built up, was the granary or barn, while to the right of the gateway the raised verandah or "Ota" was open, and here lived and slept the gate-keeper, a stalwart Purdesi, ready to challenge all incomers.

These were the stirring times which followed the Mutiny, when even the peaceful Deccan was disturbed along the Nizam's frontier by occasional inroads of gangs of freebooters. The Patel himself and his servants were well armed with matchlocks, swords, and iron-shod clubs, would doubtless have successfully resisted anything like an organised attack from without.

The Patel's so-called "kajina," or treasure chamber, was in a corner of the dwelling part of the enclosure, and was accessible only through the chief sitting-room (where the Patel transacted business) by a stout low door always well secured; it contained but two large, strong, iron-clamped chests, in one of which, when I afterwards inspected the place, there were some half-dozen bags of rupees; in the other were sundry packages of valuable ornaments done up in dirty cloths, numerous silver "lotahs" and "watees" (pots and pans), the heirlooms of the family, and a corpulent "roomal," or tied bundle of deeds and documents.

It struck me that few Government treasuries were as absolutely safe as this old Patel's strong-room, but it had its weak point, then very common in Government treasuries also—the back of the strong-room was formed by the outer wall of the main building, which abutted on one of the village lanes.

Now among the muccadums on the bridge works was a swarthy quarryman, a short, thick-set, powerful man, who, by reason of his superior intelligence and his influence among his people and fellow-workmen, had been made an overseer on the works, on the (to him) handsome salary of Rs. 30 a month. Needless to say, he also received from those under him good "dusturi" or percentage on their earnings, so that he was exceedingly well-to-do, and was far from being tempted to evil courses by want. He was also, as quarrymen go, remarkably abstemious; outwardly, in short, as respectable an old fellow (he was about sixty years of age) as one would wish to see. *But* he was descended from a long line of the old professional housebreakers of the Peishwa's time; his own father had been notoriously successful in days gone by, and it was whispered that the old fellow himself, when quite a lad—had taken part in an audacious burglary for which his father was ultimately hanged.

Jánoo Naik (as I shall call him), so far from being reticent regarding his father's exploits, was evidently proud of them, often recounting his stirring tales to an admiring audience around the evening camp fires; he enjoyed being rallied by the Patel and the leading villagers on the burglarious propensities of his family; indeed, he quite ingratiated himself with the Patel, was freely admitted into his courtyard, and actually deposited small sums for safety with him. But somehow or other he quite failed to gain the confidence of the Purdèsi gatekeeper. That surly custodian rejected all his overtures, treated him with open suspicion, and, to the great amusement of the Patel, never left his side while he was within the precincts of the courtyard—not even when he brought the greater part of his month's pay to deposit.

There was an empty outbuilding outside the Patel's "warra," or mansion, separated from it by the lane aforesaid, which led down to a watercourse, or "nullah," more or less overgrown with prickly pear. Jánoo Naik had no difficulty in persuading the Patel to let him occupy this shed with his two sons and their women folk, and they soon converted it into quite a decent adobe dwelling-house, where they all lived for nearly two years in an eminently respectable manner.

All things must have an end, even under the Public Works Department. (Remember that I am speaking of the old P. W. D. of more than a quarter of a century ago, a department that disliked unseemly haste, and was nearly as innocent of the virtues and use of Portland cement as it was of dynamite.) The bridge approached completion, many of the workmen had been discharged, and after the coming monsoon, quarrymen, lime and charcoal-burners were all to flit to the site of some fresh monument of engineering skill.

It was a sultry night in May. The villagers were for the most part sleeping for coolness' sake in their outer verandahs. The Patel and his family were reposing on charpoys in the open courtyard of his mansion, while the ever-wakeful Purdèsi was regaling himself with the grateful "hubble-bubble," occasionally giving vent to those unearthly half-coughs, half-yawns, with which these Indian guardians of the night beguile the tedium of their watch—when, in one of the few silent intervals of the baying of the village dogs, Sewram, the Purdèsi, thought he heard a dull muffled thud in the direction of the Patel's living-rooms. Laying down his pipe he went quietly over to that quarter and put his ear to the plinth.

Sure enough, he heard a regular burrowing noise right under the house!

Sewram was a very crafty and deliberate fellow. He went back to his corner, and, resuming his smoke, waited patiently until dawn, when he quietly

SEWRAM HEARS SOMETHING.

awoke the Patel and his son. The three, letting themselves noiselessly out by the half-door, walked stealthily round the corner towards Jánoo's hut—when, lo and behold, two of the women of that worthy's family were visible in the dim distance wending their way, apparently heavily laden, down towards the watercourse.

CAUGHT AT WORK.

[*To face p.* 141.

The Patel's son quietly followed them, while the Patel himself and Sewram slipped in by the open door, and, passing into a sort of inner-chamber that had been partitioned off, caught our friend Jánoo himself just emerging from a large hole in the floor! He had barely time to shout when he was secured, and the Patel and Sewram sat down screaming with laughter, to await the inevitable appearance of the two sons, who were also secured in almost less time than it has taken to tell the story. Meantime, the Patel's son returned with the two women, whom he had seen emptying bags of earth at different places among the prickly pear.

It was ultimately discovered that the highly-respectable Jánoo and his family had excavated a regular miner's gallery from their hut, under the lane, and the somewhat deep foundation of the Patel's "warra," into the warra itself. It had been quite scientifically underpinned and shored up by timbers belonging to the Public Works Department!

Jánoo and sons, of course, did the excavating, passing the earth from one to the other along the gallery, while the women carried it away and disposed of it along the bank of the watercourse. In the daytime the hole was boarded over, and Janoo's charpoy placed over it—it was really a beautiful job altogether.

We found that the gallery had pierced as far as the Patel's strong-room, and was about two feet from the surface of the floor. Another night's work would have brought it out just under the heavy treasury chest, the exact position of which the burglars, of course, did not know. It was almost a pity they had not been allowed to complete their mining operations, for when we moved the chest we found the floor already cracked underneath, and chest and all must certainly have gone through on the top of the workmen beneath.

In the burglars' hut were found plenty of housebreaking tools, and among them a very neat screwbit, nicely oiled (the property of the Sirkar Government), quite ready, when required, to bore holes round the clasps and locks of the Patel's treasure-chest. The whole of the highly-respectable family were, of course, duly sentenced to long terms of imprisonment, but the women were ultimately released on their giving us important information regarding other burglaries in distant villages, which Jánoo Naik had directed and carried out in former years.

In point of fact, Master Jánoo, following up the traditions of his ancestors, had long been the leader of a gang of burglarious quarrymen, with ramifications all over the country. The old scoundrel quite threw off the mask, I may mention, and was very proud of the whole affair, albeit its unsuccessful issue. He declared that he should never have been smothered by the chest falling through, for he had been warned by the crumbling of the earth at the head of his gallery, and had prepared stout shoring timbers and boards (which, indeed, we found in his hut), with which he should have made all safe the very next night, guessing that he must be under a chest, and had only to go on a few feet and strike upwards to find himself in the middle of the strong-room.

Neither he nor his sons would ever peach on any of their "pals," but it was afterwards found out that other quarrymen, outside the village, were accomplices, kept ready to help to carry off the booty on their pack-donkeys, and then to disperse in different directions into the jungle, where they would have buried it until opportunity offered for its removal. But "there's many a slip 'twixt cup and lip."

There is little doubt that burglars still work, though in smaller gangs, as they used to do; and the construction of the average modern native dwelling-house in India certainly does not offer much impediment to an enterprising house-breaker, nor are all watchmen as faithful or wakeful as Sewram Purdèsi, while other servants in India, as well as in England, are easy to "get at."

Wherever burglaries become rife it may be safely assumed that the police of that district are supine and inefficient. These gangs soon have their measure, and will speedily abandon a district where the police are becoming active and on the alert, for one in which the Heads of the Police are constantly being changed, the men becoming slack, easily corrupted, or hoodwinked.

There is no better test of the efficiency of the police of any district than the number of burglaries in the year, and the number in which the police have been successful. It beats all the Secretariat analyses and averages hollow; every police officer of experience knows how utterly absurd and misleading these are.

There is no reason why a fairly-remunerated police, well superintended, should not know every burglar in an Indian district as well as the Metropolitan Police know those who are constantly at work in London, and who are, invariably, sooner or later, brought to justice.

CHAPTER XV.

RIOTS.

Nothing strikes the intelligent foreign traveller in India more forcibly than the friendly and peaceable attitude of all castes and classes towards each other.

Your British "globe-trotter," especially your Parliamentary visitor, may be set down as of a different species altogether. He professes, it is true, to go out to our Eastern Empire to study the people and their wants, but it is really because he may be able the better to declaim at public meetings, or to describe them with some approach to accuracy in the pages of one or other of the hundred and one Reviews that flood the country, prepared to publish any trash, provided it bears the signature of some newly-returned tourist; but his principal aim and object is to find fault, to pick holes in the Administration, regarding which his acquaintance is of the haziest.

His knowledge of the history of our Eastern possessions is usually but a smattering, and he is utterly incapable of appreciating the difficulties which time and infinite patience have overcome. It suffices him to prime himself before he sets out on his journey on the subject of the latest grievances aired by Congress wire-pullers in London. He even hopes that he himself may be able to discover some new grievance on which to expatiate on his return. He throws himself into the arms of the Baboo and Brahmin agitators and evil-speakers; and having gorged on lies during his six weeks' or two months' peregrinations, he comes back convinced "that all the Governments in India have sold themselves to the Prince of Darkness," and forthwith poses as an authority on any Indian question of the day, whether it be the Forest enormities, the tyranny of the Police, or (as now) "the grave perils that threaten your educational interests."

French, German, and Italian travellers are usually men of a much higher type. They have already studied, and are well posted in the gradual growth of British power; they perceive the rocks that have been removed, the shoals that have been avoided; and while they are not blind to the shortcomings of our Indian Administration, they recognise, with a cordial admiration, the marvellous results they see around them. They frankly testify to the patience, prudence, perseverance, ability, and resolution with which, on the whole, the country has been, and is being, governed.

If the note-books of the numerous foreign travellers of late years in India; if the reports of the Foreign Consuls-General were available to us, we should find the fullest justice done to the Government, and its zealous and earnest servants throughout the land. They do not allow themselves to be earwigged by would-be patriot or blatant agitator; and they attach no importance to the lucubrations of the Native Press, though they marvel at the tolerance of the powers that be. Especially do they recognise the effectual control maintained everywhere by what, according to Continental notions, is the merest handful of Police and Military.

A well-known Italian traveller once borrowed from me that not very entertaining official annual, the Police Report of the Bombay Presidency for the previous year, with the express object of hereafter publishing in his own language the statistics of crime in its relation to area, population, races, and castes. In that particular year, if I remember rightly, there had not been a single riot in the whole Presidency, and he asked me if such offences against the public peace were not separately recorded in confidential reports. "It seems impossible," he observed, "that with such an entanglement of creeds and castes, there should not be perpetual friction and frequent outbursts of fanaticism." I assured him that, so far as the Western Presidency was concerned, the great Mutiny of course excluded, I could count the tumults in thirty-five years on the fingers of my two hands, and that in all India there were rarely more than a round dozen in any year, so marvellously peaceable and law-abiding is the native population.

In almost every riot Mahomedans are concerned, and usually they are the aggressors. This is natural enough, seeing how intolerant and sensitive their religion is, and how much there must be repugnant to its precepts in the daily Hindoo life and surroundings.

It is not surprising that when in certain years a noisy Hindoo festival occurs at the same time as a solemn Mahomedan fast, the devout followers of the Prophet should be scandalised and finally lose patience. The wonder is, that these collisions are not much more common than they are, and much more dangerous. I am reminded of such an occasion in the early Sixties, when, though there was no actual loss of life, there was plenty of bloodshed, and there would probably have been a very serious outbreak, but for the accidental presence on the spot of an energetic young Civilian.

It was the Mahomedan fast of the Ramzan, and on the same night was to be a "palki," or palanquin procession of some Hindoo deity in the town of Dajipur. The Mahomedan element was strong in the town, but there had never been the least ill-feeling between Mahomedans and Hindoos before, and there was not the least reason to anticipate that it would be excited on this particular occasion. No precautions had ever been considered necessary, and I therefore took none, nor had I any reason for leaving other important duty to guard against a breach of the peace at Dajipur, forty miles from my camp.

I was drinking my early tea next morning, when the Patel, in a great state of excitement, came up to my tent, stating that a Mhar messenger had come in from a neighbouring village with a report that there had been a bloody fight at Dajipur during the night, between the Mahomedans and the Hindoos, in which several of the latter, as well as the Foujdar, had been killed; that a young Saheb there had ordered the Police to fire on the mob, and had shot one man after he had himself been severely wounded about the head; that the Mahomedans were trying to break into the Mamlutdar's "Kacheri," or Office, where the Saheb aforesaid was shut up with the Treasury Guards.

I lost no time, of course, in starting for Dajipur, where I found that young D——, recently appointed Income-tax Commissioner of the District, was in the "Kacheri," the big gate of which had been fastened to keep out an excited mob, who crowded round me, clamouring that the Saheb had "murdered" a man whose body he had got inside. I confess I *was* relieved when D—— (with his face tied up) let me in at the gate, and burst out laughing when I asked him where the dead man was. He took me to the guard-room, where a strapping Mahomedan was squatted, moaning as he nursed his bandaged leg, he then proceeded to tell the whole story while I discussed the excellent "tiffin" he set before me.

I must here mention that the town of Dajipur is built along the bank of what is a tolerably large river during the monsoon, the bed of which, however, was nearly dry at that season. The Mamlutdar's Kacheri (or offices—Dajipur is the headquarters of a "taluka," or sub-district) is in an old fort, over the gateway of which is a small room in which European

District Officers in those days usually put up when visiting the place on duty. This fort is on the bank opposite to the town, to which there is only access by a distant Mahratta bridge in the monsoon. At other seasons it is easily crossed by huge stepping-stones laid in the bed of the shallow stream.

D—— had arrived at the town the day before, went straight to the gateway room, and worked hard at income-tax work till 10 P.M., when he went to bed, thoroughly tired out, falling fast asleep, regardless of the din of "tom-toms" and all kinds of native music in the town across the river. About eleven o'clock he was awakened by a light in his eyes, to find the Brahmin Foujdar (or chief constable, as he is now called) and some armed Police round his bed.

In a great state of perturbation they besought him as a Magistrate to come over to the town with them to try to quell a row that had broken out between the Hindoos and the Mahomedans, in consequence of the former having carried the palanquin of their god along the main street past a mosque where the Faithful were at solemn prayer. D—— accordingly buckled on his revolver, took a stick, and, lighted by torches, crossed the river bed with all the Police available (eight or ten in number), after leaving three men to guard the Treasury.

The main street of Dajipur is very narrow, and there are numerous even narrower passages leading down to the riverside. Down one of these passages, and about twenty or thirty yards from the main street, was a small mosque, but all access to it was

THE RIOT. [*To face p.* 151.

crowded by excited Moslems, shouting "Deen, Deen," and striving to smash up the sacred palanquin, which, however, was being stoutly defended by the bearers and a few sturdy Mahrattas. The whole scene was dimly lighted by two or three torches, and "as pretty a row going on," said D——, "as you'd wish to see in Ireland."

The arrival of the Police with a real live Saheb caused a momentary lull, of which D—— and the Foujdar took advantage, by drawing the Police up across the neck of the lane, or passage, leading down to the mosque; the Mahomedans were thus confined more or less to the lane, and separated from their Hindoo prey in the main street. The Police fixed bayonets, and D—— and the Foujdar went down the lane towards the mosque to accost a leading Syed, or holy man, who was evidently trying to keep the Moslems quiet.

They had scarcely time to utter a few words, however, when the shouts of "Deen, Deen" broke out afresh, and a tremendous shower of stones came from the lower and dark end of the lane. The Foujdar received one large boulder on the kneecap, D—— had his helmet knocked off, and several of the Police were hit. They charged down the lane two or three times very pluckily, but could not catch any of their assailants, and whenever they formed up again they were again pelted mercilessly with stones.

At last the Mahomedans summoned up courage to make a determined rush to get through the Police line at the Hindoos with the palanquin (these worthies, by the way, never tried to help their defenders); they charged right up to the bayonets, only retreating when two or three of them received slight flesh wounds. D—— shouted to the Police to fire blank cartridge (strictly in accordance with the standing orders of the recent troublous times). A volley was fired, but with no other result than to infuriate the mob, some of whom nearly succeeded in wresting muskets from the Police, while D—— was struck over the jaw by a club, and stunned for the moment. Pulling himself together, however, he tried to seize a rioter in front of him, when several others turned back with uplifted clubs; he then drew his revolver, and, aiming low, fired two shots into the "brown of them," dropping one man, who, however, was immediately lifted up and carried down a dark passage. The Police rushed to his side, and D—— then gave the word to load with ball, which was done; but the rioters were already cowed, and contented themselves with throwing stones and yelling at intervals as they gradually dispersed along the river bed and in the neighbouring lanes and passages.

D—— and the Foujdar, nastily bruised as he was, stayed until the Hindoos had carried off their palanquin, and the town seemed quite deserted, when they returned to the Kacheri Fort, and the three Police on guard over the Treasury were despatched to the nearest posts for further assistance, which arrived at daybreak.

The Foujdar and the Police with D—— had

recognised many of their assailants and other rioters, but, of course, these gentlemen were not to be found next day. In the meantime D—— was very anxious to find the man he had dropped, but nothing was heard of him till just before I arrived, when the guard at the Fort Gate reported that a small crowd was crossing the river, and that they carried a man on a litter.

Arrangements were accordingly made, so that directly the litter and bearers were within the gateway it was promptly shut and secured; and there, sure enough, was D——'s victim, who was declared by the excited friends and relatives who carried him to be at the point of death; in fact, said they, "We have come to lodge information against the Saheb there, who is his murderer." D—— seeing the fellow was not much hurt, insisted on seeing the wound, which proved to be a flesh wound in the calf of the leg, the bullet (a small one) having run round the bone and being plainly visible on the surface near the shin.

D—— tried to persuade the man to have a ligature tied above and below, and let the barber make an incision through which the bullet would fly out; but neither he nor his relatives would allow it, the latter insisting that he would soon die. D—— at last told his friends he should keep the man prisoner until an escort could be provided to take him to the nearest civil hospital (some fifty miles off)—he had just turned the relatives out of the Fort when I appeared on the scene.

I sent the wounded man off next day, the bullet was easily extracted, and he was well enough in a few days to take his place among forty-two out of nearly one hundred and fifty accused, about whose identification there could be no doubt. They were in due course convicted before the District Magistrate, who sentenced them to a year's hard labour a-piece and three hundred rupees fine, or, in default, three months more.

I may mention that D——, besides several severe contusions on the head and body, had all the back teeth on one side of his face broken, while the Foujdar was *hors de combat* for some months, and several of the Police, and about a dozen Hindoos, were a good deal knocked about by stones.

In compliance with special orders issued towards the end of the days of the Mutiny, and not then cancelled, D—— and I made special reports of what had occurred direct to the Private Secretary to the Governor. In due course D—— was officially informed that, while his Excellency the Governor in Council was of opinion that the use of firearms was absolutely necessary and justifiable on this occasion, his Excellency regretted that Mr. D—— "should have emulated the Police!" How D—— did swear on receiving this wigging, and how I did laugh at him! Certain it is that if D—— had not dropped that man just when he did, and shown that he meant business afterwards, there would have been a very serious tumult, in which, in all probability, D——

and several Police and Hindoos would have lost their lives.

Most Police Officers of experience will, I fancy, agree with me that, under any circumstances and with any mob, firing blank cartridge is utterly useless; with an excited Mahomedan mob, already arrived at the "Deen, Deen" stage, it is worse than useless, for the rioters do not in the least comprehend this way of reading the Riot Act, and only fancy you are afraid to use ball.* A Hindoo mob in ordinary times can be safely tackled with sticks, but a Mussulman mob is always dangerous, and when it comes to "Deen, Deen," sharp and decisive action is imperatively needed, and you should aim low and let drive into the "brown of them."

There are exceptions, however, to every rule, and the so-called Broach Riots on the 22nd November, 1885, furnished a proof that other than Mahomedan mobs can sometimes be very dangerous.

The first report of what had happened was to the effect that an ascetic Talavia, having failed to obtain a site for a temple which it is alleged had been promised to his people, went with a mob to the Collector's bungalow to obtain redress. On their way they met Mr. Prescott, the Police Superintendent, stopped his dog-cart, and beat him so severely about the head with sticks that he died in a couple of hours.

Excited by the sight of the blood they had shed,

* The use of blank cartridge has been prohibited by the Government of India since the above was written.

and the strength of their force having been increased by fresh arrivals, they next attacked the police "chowkies," and, obtaining arms, went off to loot the Bank, where they were repulsed. In the meantime, the Police collected and followed them up, and a fight ensued, in the course of which four of the Police were wounded and five of the rioters were shot dead.

This is the substance of what was first telegraphed to Bombay; but it came out at the trial of many Talavias subsequently arrested, that, as a matter of fact, the leaders of these lunatics actually contemplated a rebellion against the British Raj, and had for many days assembled their followers, and deliberately planned an outbreak which was prematurely brought to a head by their unexpected meeting with poor Mr. Prescott.

The lesson to be learnt from this lamentable case is, that gatherings of ignorant and fanatical sects or tribes or castes, for however seemingly harmless purposes, should not be permitted anywhere, under any circumstances.

As to the disputes so common at the Mohurrum, regarding the customary rights of processionists, the best, if not the only way to deal with them, when a breach of the peace seems probable, is for the authorities to do as Sir Barrow Ellis always did when he was an Assistant Collector and Magistrate—to prohibit them altogether, until both parties appear together and formally declare that they have amicably settled their differences.

It is the function of the Magistracy to take these reasonable precautions; and the less Police Officers inquire into the merits of disputes, or attempt to decide upon the rights of the parties, the better for all concerned. When an unforeseen collision occurs, the establishment of a punitive post is the best remedy against its recurrence; but it is a remedy that is apt to bear harshly on comparatively innocent persons, and ought not to be adopted without much previous consideration.

Most Police Officers will agree with me in cordially acknowledging the assistance they always receive from the leaders of the Mahomedan community in all endeavours to effect an amicable settlement of differences, whether among their co-religionists or between them and other disputants.

NOTE.—Since this chapter was written the great Cow-Riots have occurred in various parts of India, notably in Bombay. Lord Lansdowne's allusions to them in one of his latest public speeches at Calcutta are very much to the point.

His Lordship said : "I should not be doing my duty if I did not refer to another symptom, which seems to me to be alarming and to deserve our earnest attention. I refer to the increased bitterness of feeling manifested between the two great religious denominations. The policy of the Government of India in these matters has been one of strict neutrality and of sympathy with that side, whether it be Hindoo or Mahomedan, which desires to observe its customary ritual, and expects to be allowed to do so in peace. I have lately spoken at length upon this subject, and I will not pursue it now. The whole question has been very thoroughly examined, and our mature conclusions will be submitted to my successor. I feel sure that nothing will be done rashly or under the influence of panic. I should strongly deprecate any extensive or radical changes in the law, until it has been demonstrated that the existing law is powerless to deal with these evils. I would infinitely prefer to rely upon the good sense and moderation of the people themselves and upon vigorous and determined executive action based upon the law as it now exists, than upon special legislation ; and I am not without hopes that both sides have now realised the folly of their conduct, and will join us in discouraging similar exhibitions of sectional hatred and lawlessness."

CHAPTER XVI.

FOREST ROBBERIES.

I AM one of those who have always felt the deepest sympathy for the earnest, zealous, hard-working Forest Department. Forest Officers have always been among the best abused of officials. Even the Police have not had such hard measure dealt out to them by the public at large, while their treatment by the Government they serve so admirably has been capricious, unjust, and unreasonable to a degree.

There are probably not many men now in India who remember the good old times when the forests, like a good many other matters—salt, excise, and even customs—were left a good deal to chance; when "Bombay Castle" possessed but the foggiest knowledge of the precise position of the valuable properties belonging to the State, and certainly had no accurate register of them; when the idea of conservation, still less of afforestation for the benefit of posterity, never entered the brain of Chief Secretary, Revenue Commissioner, or Collector; when, so long as sufficient timber was sent up to the Bombay Dockyard, and enough money scraped together spasmodically to nearly cover the scanty pay of one or two

Conservators, and a few (a *very* few) clerks and peons, "His Excellency the Governor in Council" was perfectly satisfied, and was content to pigeonhole with calm indifference the valuable reports, full of earnest warnings, teeming with practical suggestions, annually submitted by able men like "Daddy Gibson" and Dalzell.

"The world went very well then" for those who needed wood for any purpose. Did an energetic Collector or Assistant-Collector want timber for a school or a dhurm-salla (rest-house), he simply ordered the Mamlutdar (Head Revenue and Magisterial Officer of a sub-district) to send out and have it cut. Did an officer of the Roads and Tanks Department want charcoal, he sent his men out and hacked and burnt and wasted as he chose. Did a villager, from the Patel downwards, want wood for any purpose, he simply helped himself, while timber-merchants and boat-builders with perfect impunity pillaged right and left, and the forest tribes gradually denuded the hillsides around large towns, living by the sale of firewood, which cost them nothing but the labour of felling and taking away. The actual loss to the State by this reckless waste, in the first thirty-five years after the downfall of the Peishwa, must have been many crores of rupees, but it is but a fraction of the loss to the present generation of the people at large, as sensible men among them now perceive.

This sinful waste went on till the early Fifties, when the administration throughout India began to entertain some glimmering of the vast importance of forest conservation in the future. But the first remedial steps had hardly been taken when the country was convulsed by the Mutiny and Rebellion, and reforms in this and many another important direction had, perforce, to be laid aside till quieter times, so that it was not really till about 1863, if I remember aright, that a Forest Department was regularly organised, even then it was very indifferently equipped.

Meantime enormous mischief had been prepared for the future in the widespread growth of a belief among the people that they possessed, or had acquired, prescriptive rights to devastate the forests at their own sweet will. Restrictions, however reasonable and just, were regarded as "zoolum," spoliation, or the mere exercise of arbitrary power. This dangerous feeling especially predominated in the Bombay Presidency, and in the country all around the Presidency city; for, what with the marvellous impetus given to trade in the early Sixties, what with the introduction of Vehar water, the population of Bombay had nearly doubled, and with it the demand for fuel.

Thousands of men, mostly sturdy "Ghattis,"* had gradually formed into hundreds of gangs felling firewood wherever it could be found within paying distance of the city, to which it was transported by rail, carts, and native boats. While yet un-

* Marattas from along the Ghauts, or Syhádri Range of Mountains.

M

prepared and insufficiently manned, the unfortunate Forest Department, now incessantly called upon by Government to show good financial results, had to combat combination after combination, to check petty thieving as well as to repress wholesale organised robbery, at the same time to prevent clamour, and to see that the city was fully supplied with fuel at a reasonable rate. How devotedly the Department worked, how well on the whole it succeeded, must be fresh in the recollection of all old Bombay residents. Indifferent to the abuse showered on it from all sides, not discouraged by the niggardliness and the contradictory orders from time to time issued from the Secretariat, the heads of the Department gradually systematised the supply to Bombay, arranged for block-felling by rotation and supervised the felling by their own officers.

It was about this time some seventeen years ago, that the following remarkable case occurred. It will, in all likelihood, be remembered by sundry and various officials in the Western Presidency, notwithstanding the care that will be taken here to conceal names and localities. I was not myself in any way officially connected with it, but I was favoured by a brother "peeler" with a perusal of his notes, from which I took some of my own sufficient to enable me to give an outline of the main facts.

Great pressure was at the time being brought to bear on the Forest Officer of a district not far from Bombay to raise an extra amount of revenue to cover the cost of certain much-needed supplementary establishments which Government had with much difficulty been induced to sanction. He was therefore driven to fell more firewood jungle than usual, which necessitated the employment of contractors instead of felling departmentally. These contractors were, I well remember, restricted to cutting the commoner kinds of fuel trees, the better or building timbers, such as "Teak," "Ain," "Kinjal," being expressly excepted by the terms of the contract. The contractors bound themselves to fell so many thousand "candies"—about 688 lbs.—of wood in certain specified jungles, to remove it after cutting it into billets, to certain convenient depôts outside the forests, and then to buy it at a certain rate per "candy," with permission to remove it by pack-bullocks or by tidal creeks to the nearest railway station, or to the city of Bombay itself.

With efficient supervision over the axe-men and common honesty at the depôts, the contracts, though loosely worded, might have worked fairly well, saving the Department enormous labour, and in a rough and ready way netting a fair return. But the supervision unfortunately, could not be efficient, and this from no fault or want of energy on the part of superior Forest Officials. Besides routine office duties, and having to travel over an immense area of rugged country, the unfortunate Assistant Conservator was in those days expected to do something towards forest demarcation, a duty which in itself takes up the whole time of any hard-working man. He could not be in two places at once, and was compelled to rely on his subordinates, depôt-keepers, and the like. Once these gentry became the tools of the contractors, any amount of depredation could be carried on with impunity, almost without the least risk of discovery; and that was what happened on this occasion.

The contractors were simply some twenty stalwart "Ghattis," every one of whom for years past, and their fathers before them, had exploited forest lands for the supply of Bombay. The "Company"—"Ballaji Ghatti and Co.," as they called themselves—had very little money of their own, probably not more than two to five hundred rupees a-piece, except Ballaji, who having a thousand to contribute to the capital, and being moreover a man of exceptional energy and force of character, was naturally the chief manager or director. Ballaji's and his brother's share in the venture was, I think, eight annas in the rupee. It was he who did the financing; it was his brother who kept the books; the other members of the so-called Company were merely working gangers or muccadums, with half-anna, quarter-anna, or pie shares in the profits in proportion to the amount of capital they each brought in.

Of course the Company had backers in Bombay; for a big contract like this, likely to run for two or three years, requires considerable capital to start and carry on with until the wood can reach the market and be sold. Several months must elapse before wood cut in the jungles during the monsoon is even fit for sale. Meantime axe-men and labourers have to be paid. "Brinjaris" (Indian gypsies, or men with droves of pack-bullocks) have to be given advances at the outset and kept paid from month to month, while their droves of pack-bullocks toil dustily and wearily backwards and forwards, from jungle to depôt, removing the logs; cartmen or boatmen, or (as in this instance) both, have to be paid cash down for all the wood transported to Bombay.

Ballaji Ghatti and Co.'s backers were wealthy wood dealers at Carnac Bunder; who when Ballaji had secured this contract, were quite ready and able to advance the Company all moneys required, on a stamped agreement that all the wood worked by it should be consigned or sent to them at Carnac Bunder. The backers, whom I will call Haji Ladak and Co., had also power under the deed to inspect Ballaji's books, and if necessary, even to overlook the operations up-country.

Thus amply provided with capital, Ballaji Ghatti and Co. set merrily to work, felling an immense supply of fuel ready for removal after the monsoon. It was a very easy matter to corrupt the depôt-keepers and the few rangers concerned. Regular pay, perhaps twice as much as the pittance paid to them by the Government, secured their hearty co-operation in the extensive frauds that followed. The depôt-keepers simply had to shut their eyes, let as much wood as Ballaji and Co. chose to bring down pass through and out of the depôt, being careful only to keep their books in tally with the dummy set of books kept by the firm to show to the "Assistant Saheb," or any one desirous of learning what progress was being made under the contract.

The firm's *real* books, of course, corresponded as to consignments and advances with those of the consignees and backers, Haji Ladak and Co., which, I may mention in passing, were as truly and honestly kept as those of any large firm in Bombay.

The forest ranger had merely to hold his tongue and ignore the felling of teak and other timber excluded from the contract. If the "Saheb" happened to come along—there was always ample warning—for a day or two few pack-bullocks would be seen about, and the sound of the axe would scarcely be heard on the hill-sides. The villagers round about, liberally supplied by Ballaji with brushwood and such occasional pieces of timber as they required, did not peach and all went happily as a marriage-bell.

Ballaji Ghatti and Co. were coining money by thousands monthly; believing they were quite safe, they extended their operations and boldly stacked great wood piles at any spot convenient for removal, especially on the banks of certain small tidal creeklets navigable by small native craft. It was, I believe, ascertained subsequently that Government was robbed under this contract to the tune of nearly two lakhs of rupees in about three years, and the depredations would probably never have been checked had not an exceptionally sharp Parsi inspector of police been appointed to the district.

SECRET FOREST HOARDS. [*To face p.* 166.

Ruttonjee, now dead some years, used to be called by his European superiors Inspector "Bucket,"* so much did he remind them in manner and appearance of that plausible detective. It was not long before he smelt a rat, and set himself to work to ferret out all the details of the plot. He first easily ingratiated himself with Ballaji and Co., wormed all he could out of them, got a sight of the contract,

INSPECTOR "BUCKET."

and] plied some of the "Ghatti" partners with liquor on every possible occasion, when they let out the secret of the double sets of books, and boasted freely of their gains. Going to Bombay he scraped acquaintance through mutual friends

* Charles Dickens's 'Bleak House.'

with Haji Ladak and Co., and thoroughly satisfied himself that he was in for a "real good thing;" then, making some police pretence for passing a few days in one of the jungles being felled, he saw with his own eyes two immense stacks of wood of all kinds ready for removal.

His next step was to take the opportunity of the Police Superintendent dining one night quietly with the Collector and District Magistrate to wait upon them and divulge the conspiracy. These gentlemen, in the absence of the Assistant Conservator of Forests (who was too far off), determined to strike at once. By the following evening all the forest depôts where Ballaji and Co. were working, all the great wood piles in the jungles and most of the books, were in the charge of the Police.

Unfortunately, Ballaji, who had the true books of the firm over in Bombay, somehow received intelligence in time to enable him to secrete them, so that they were not found till after the trial. The District Magistrate undertook the investigation himself, Ruttonjee prosecuting; in due course Ballaji, his brother, and I think a dozen more "Ghattis," signatories to the Company's deed of partnership, who had been actively engaged in supervising operations in the forests, were committed for trial to the Sessions, on charges of stealing teak and other valuable timbers, besides the huge wood piles found in the jungles.

The Crown was represented at the trial by an English barrister of high standing, and also one of the leading native pleaders of the High Court. The case seemed simple enough : the contract permitted the accused to fell and remove a certain quantity of fuel wood ; but Haji Ladak's evidence and the books of his firm showed that the accused had already delivered in Bombay and received credit for about twenty times as much as the stipulated quantity, besides that they were in possession of half as much more stacked in the jungles.

The contract forbade the accused to cut teak and other specified building timbers, but it was proved that they had nevertheless felled such timber, transported it to Bombay and sold it, besides stacking much more ready for removal.

For the defence, which was conducted by two astute native pleaders, it was contended that a criminal charge could not lie : that the Government remedy, if any existed, was a suit for damages for breach of contract. The false or dummy books of Ballaji Ghatti and Co., and the several depôt-keepers' books above mentioned, were relied upon as proving that the Company had not felled or removed more than they were entitled to under the contract ; it was further contended that the excess shown in Haji Ladak's books was purchased in the course of trade from various other parties ; that the wood piles found in the jungles were not actually found in the possession of the accused, but must have been stored by some other persons unknown.

The Judge decided that under any circumstances the charge of theft would not apply, and the accused were acquitted. On this, Government appealed to the High Court, against the acquittal, so far as Ballaji and his brother were concerned, the accomplices not being considered worth the trouble. An appeal against an acquittal is no common occurrence. A Full Court of the Honourable Judges, after a patient hearing, reversed the acquittal, found these two men guilty, and passed a moderate sentence.

I am afraid that, in the above sketch of the case from memory, I may have omitted several points, especially some of a legal nature; but my object has been rather to show how the State used to be defrauded in forest matters, how serious were the obstacles which opposed the strenuous exertions of the department in the earlier days of its organisation, than to describe accurately the details of a trial which attracted considerable attention at the time. It can easily be selected by the curious from among the reported cases of the High Court of Judicature of about 1875-76.

As time has gone on the Government has become juster and more liberal in its grants towards a most important department, its organisation has steadily improved, excellent checks on fraud and depredation have been put in force, and such conspiracies as that of Ballaji Ghatti and Co. have become well-nigh impossible.

The sequel to the case is well worth telling. "Inspector Bucket" was excessively annoyed at the "Ghattis" having been enabled to get their real books out of the way, and he vowed that he would never rest until he traced them. It was not, however, till several months had elapsed that, obtaining a clue, he actually unearthed them in the house of a relative of Ballaji; proceedings were thereupon instituted against certain members of the old Company for producing the fictitious books in evidence at the Sessions trial, of whom in the result two or three more were convicted and sentenced.

Poor Ruttonjee would undoubtedly have risen to the highest grades in the Police Service, but that his eyesight totally failed him when he had reached the Inspector grade; not having served sufficiently long for a pension, I fear, he died in very poor circumstances.

"TIM" ON DUTY.

CHAPTER XVII.

THE PREDATORY TRIBES.

EVERY one serving in India in the early "Fifties" must retain a vivid recollection of the kind of lull that then prevailed throughout the length and breadth of the land—the lull before the storm.

It was in those days that the Court of Directors first bethought themselves of making some general and sustained effort to suppress crime; the Indian Governments were urged to improve the organisation of the Police, to trace out the swarms of thieves who infested the country, who, not only by their own predatory habits, but by reason of their close connection with "Thugs," "dacoits," cattle-lifters, and poisoners, rendered the detection and suppression of more serious crimes well-nigh impossible.

The Thuggee Suppression Department of the Government of India was naturally employed in a systematic investigation of the habits, customs, and mode of operation of the hundred-and-one predatory castes and tribes scattered throughout the Deccan and the Carnatic. Captain (now General) Hervey, an experienced officer of the department in the Southern Mahratta Country, with the aid of Thug approvers, devoted some years of patient labour to the classification of Bamptias, Oochlias, Kaikaris, Katkaris, Wadars, Beldars, besides a host of musicians, jugglers, mummers, and acrobats, all of whom preyed upon hapless villagers, some openly, some under the cloak of an ostensible occupation. His report, so far as I am aware, has been the only text-book or work of reference for nearly forty years, and he has done well to publish a new book in the past year.

Although these tribes are fast dwindling away, or being absorbed in the labouring population, and they are no longer the scourge to the country they used to be, or because of police viligance are now comparatively harmless, their organisations remain, their old traditions are religiously preserved, it is quite certain that if circumstances again favoured their operations, they would again give an infinity of trouble to the authorities. General Hervey's work should, therefore, be found in the official library of every District Magistrate and Police officer in the Western and Southern Presidencies.

Veriest dregs of the population as they are, they attracted little special notice during disturbed times anterior to British rule; they were merged in the swarms of camp-followers and hangers-on to every native army, to every Pindari horde, or considerable band of marauders, and as the country settled down, they crystallised as it were, into small bands and gangs, and spread far and wide among the villages.

Vast numbers of them, such as the Wadars (earth-workers), Beldars (quarrymen), lime and charcoal-burners, basket-makers, have been more or less permanently absorbed into the great body of migratory labour required for the construction of roads and railways, canals and tanks, during the past thirty years.

Thousands upon thousands of them were swept off by famine and cholera between 1876 and 1880. Comparatively few gangs still remain to wander about the Deccan, and there is now little or nothing in their appearance or habits to distinguish one tribe from another. The malodorous but somewhat picturesque procession of old crones, bold-faced slatternly girls, and nearly-naked urchins occasionally encountered on the road, with its drove of donkeys and buffaloes heavily laden with mats and hut-poles, on which are perched a few dissipated-looking fowls, may belong to any tribe. They eat any garbage—land-crabs, field rats, village pigs, or what not. They all drink like fishes when they get a chance, but yet one tribe will not eat, or drink, or intermarry with another, so scrupulously are caste distinctions observed among them.

They frequent every fair and jattra (pilgrimage), where they annex every portable thing they can lay their hands upon, pilfer from every shop-keeper's stall, and finally decamp at night with goats or sheep which they promptly eat, or with a few head of cattle, which some of the men drive rapidly off to a distant town and sell for anything they will fetch. On their way from fair to fair, from "jattra" to "jattra," they will sometimes squat for a few weeks together on the outskirts of some town or village where any building operations are in progress, and they get fairly well paid for fetching sand, or earth, or chunan (lime) with their long-suffering donkeys.

Neither these poor beasts nor the buffaloes are ever fed. The day's work or the day's march over, they are simply turned loose to forage for themselves in the crops if they are standing, in the stackyards or around the threshing-floors if the harvest is over. The villagers well know that it is hopeless to attempt to catch the cunning beasts at night, for some time they patiently tolerate the nuisance, but the usual ending is a free fight, when the Ryots, exasperated beyond endurance, turn out some morning and drive their rascally visitors beyond the village limits.

I remember witnessing an affair of this kind some

years ago, which gave me a fair idea of the omnivorous dishonesty of these wandering rogues. It was early dawn, accompanied by a couple of sowars (mounted police), I was on my way to inspect a police post at some distance from my camp. As we were passing a small walled village that stood back from the road, shouts and screams broke the silence. Galloping towards the village we came upon an encampment of Khaikaris (ostensibly basket-makers), in which, amid a cloud of dust, some twenty sturdy Mahrattas, armed with sticks, were demolishing the filthy mat hovels and freely belabouring the male occupants.

The shrill shrieks of the women, the yelping of curs, the imprecations of the combatants, the donkeys and cattle rushing wildly about in the middle, made up as pretty a scrimmage as has ever been witnessed outside Donnybrook. The unexpected appearance of a "Saheb" on the scene, perhaps a few cracks from my horsewhip, produced a momentary calm, and then a crowd of Khaikari women rushed forward, beating their breasts, vociferating and pointing to a female lying apparently senseless near.

Dismounting to see what was the matter with her, and giving my horse to a sowar to hold, that worthy told me, with a broad grin, that the woman was only shamming, and that he had seen her cast herself down on the ground as we rode up.

However, as she persisted in feigning to be dead, I ordered a "chatty" of cold water to be brought, and myself drenched her with the contents. Needless to say the effect was magical. The crone jumped up, and proceeded to curse me volubly by all her gods, amid roars of laughter from the assembled villagers.

Putting a cordon of Mhars (village watchmen) round the encampment, I held a rough-and-ready inquiry. It was the old story. The gang had arrived about a week before from Punderpoor, pitched their camp without permission, and refused to budge when ordered by the Patel. Their beasts had been turned loose every night to graze their fill in the standing wheat; calves and goats had disappeared; houses and shops had been robbed right and left; and last, but not least, the behaviour of the younger Khaikari women had been scandalously indecent, so the incensed village elders had determined at last to rid themselves forcibly of their unwelcome visitors.

Gravely reproving them (as in duty bound) for having taken the law into their own hands, but secretly in my own heart, approving what they had done, I proceeded to have the huts and every member of the gang of Khaikaris thoroughly searched. Never was such a wonderful collection of spoil found! Some half-dozen pieces of well-worn silver jewellery, several bundles of brand-new brass ornaments, ear and nose rings, bangles and necklaces, bunches of coloured beads, several little circular folding-mirrors, new tin pots, plates, pans, new and old copper and brass "lotahs," coils of new rope and balls of string, embroidered skull-caps, women's brass back-combs, breast cloths, "saris," or petticoats, new "Dhoturs," pieces of cotton cloth and sandals "kumblis" (blankets), tied in the middle and filled with grain and pulse of all kinds. Besides all this miscellaneous "loot," the men had some fifty rupees in cash concealed about their persons. It was plain enough that the gang had had a real good time at Punderpoor.

Some few articles being identified by the villagers, I sent the whole gang back to the Punderpoor Native Magistrate, who ultimately convicted about half of them. I was not surprised to learn six months afterwards, that the stackyard of this particular village had been fired and grievous loss inflicted on the unhappy ryots (cultivators). Of course this was a piece of revenge perpetrated by some members of the gang, who probably travelled many miles for the purpose. These rogues always manage to pay out any village that may have offended them, which is doubtless one of the reasons they are tolerated so patiently. Moreover their old women are credited with the evil eye, and believed to practise witchcraft extensively.

It is a very difficult problem to know how to deal with these wandering rogues; they do not mind being "moved on," for they are always more or less on the move, they are quite indifferent where they go, so long as they can manage to get to the next "jattra," wherever it may be. The police are not numerous enough to follow them up, the people rarely lodge a complaint against them for the reasons above given, thus there are no specific grounds for interfering with them.

There are other predatory tribes, not migratory, of whom the "Bamptias" and "Oochlias" of the Deccan may be regarded as types. They have no ostensibly honest means of livelihood, they are thieves pure and simple as their tribal names explain. "Oochlia," for example, is derived from the verb "Oochalnè," to lift or pick up. In former years they usually inhabited a quarter of their own in every considerable town; villages they did not care about; there was no scope in them for the exercise of their great talents for theft on an extensive scale.

The old native "raj" strove hard to rid the principal cities of the pest, and even to reclaim these people from their predatory habits; they were driven out of the towns and compelled to live on sites allotted to them, lands were given over for their cultivation, advances of cash, occasionally regular cash allowances, were granted to them for the purchase of seed and cattle and implements of husbandry. There was at least one "Bamptia" village close to Poona itself, and for aught I know it may still exist. They were also numerous in the Satara and Kolhapur territories, and in the petty Mahratta States, but the experiment never succeeded very well in any of them, though no doubt it was an advantage to have the rascals collected together at spots where they could be subjected to some kind of discipline and supervision, such as being compelled to attend muster at least at nightfall, and once earlier in the day. Some few certainly have settled down into fairly honest cultivators, but the majority of them, from father to son, are still regularly brought up and carefully trained to steal, and as I shall presently explain, a splendid and boundless field has opened out for them of late years.

They are exceedingly intelligent and observant, very active in their habits, the lads being as carefully trained in running and athletic exercises as they are trained in the skilful use of their fingers. They are good actors and able to assume almost any disguise; very plausible and insinuating in their address, scrupulously clean in their persons and habits, and somewhat addicted to finery withal. They rarely drink: their womenkind, all expert thieves themselves, have or had a reputation for virtue. They are very staunch to each other, no police officer ever succeeded in getting any reliable information out of a "Bamptia." They rarely molest their immediate neighbours, do not steal sheep, goats, or cattle, or pilfer from shopkeepers in the vicinity of their homes. In fact, they pay freely and honestly for what they want, are willing to do a good turn for a neighbour, and generally are thought rather good fellows than otherwise.

Travellers have always been, and always will be, their prey, but they never resort to violence, and I never heard of their taking human life. They are to be found very busy in the dense crowds thronging into a sacred shrine, detaching the heavy silver "Kirgutis" (waist-belts) or long cotton-bag purses carried by well-to-do Mahrattas, or snipping off necklaces and earrings, which they pass from hand to hand with incredible rapidity. If there is a row, or one of them is suspected when an article is missed, he does not run away, but assumes a virtuously indignant air, it is very certain nothing will be found upon him. "Pandoorang Hari" relates many amusing tales of their tricks upon travellers, but none of them beats the story I am going to tell about myself.

Pray remember, good reader, while you laugh at me, that when the incident happened I was a very young policeman indeed. Marching between Satara and Kholapur, I halted for a couple of days' shooting at a favourite camp within hail of one of these "Oochlia" villages. Being full of zeal, as all young "Peelers" should be, and withal rather fond of airing my Mahratta on every possible occasion, I sent for two or three of the elders from the "Oochlia" hamlet in the evening, and had a long and very affable conversation with them.

They were pleasant and unreserved about the lives their people used to lead under the *former* or native "raj," but *they* of course had long since abandoned all dishonest practices, and had settled down as honest cultivators. They were doing very well—were bringing up their children in the paths of virtue, indeed they were about to petition the Sirkar to let them have a school. Under the Company's "raj" thieving could not prosper, while every honest man was safe and happy. "No one knew better than the Saheb, whose knowledge of the language and of the native character was notorious throughout the country." I sucked it all in greedily like the young fool I was, promised to say a good word for the school and we parted the very best of friends. After a frugal meal and the pipe of peace, I inducted myself into my "pyjamas" and went to bed, feeling particularly well satisfied with myself, and firmly convinced that I was the most promising young policeman in the Presidency.

I was always I must mention much given to dogs, and at that time possessed two—one, Vickie, a little black-and-tan terrier who always slept on my bed, the other a huge bull-dog, very good tempered when loose, but a perfect demon when on the chain. "Tim" always travelled with the cook, being chained at night to the "Bobbajikhana," or cook's cart, under which he slept a few yards from the fire, my two servants sleeping near. We were all very tired and the camp was soon buried in sleep, when I was suddenly awakened by the most horrible yell from the fire. Springing off the bed and catching up a stick, I rushed to the spot to find the faithful "Tim" holding on to the leg of a nearly naked lad of about sixteen, who was screaming "Murder" at the top of his voice.

Needless to say, all the little camp gathered on the spot. The first thing was to get "Tim" to release his hold of the lad's leg—no easy matter to accomplish, for "Tim" had got his teeth well in above the ankle. The boy bled profusely, and was half dead with fright. We dressed the wound, gave him some brandy and tried to get the young rascal to tell us

[To face p. 182.

THE NIGHT'S SURPRISE: "TIM'S GOT HIM."

how and why he came there, but he simply would not open his mouth. There was nothing for it but to tie him hand and foot, and leave him in charge of my solitary peon (I was not allowed a sentry in those early days), with strict injunctions not to go to sleep again.

I then ordered a "peg" (brandy-and-soda) to be brought to my tent, and returned to have a smoke before turning in again. Lo and behold! my tent had been fairly cleaned out; the clothes I had taken off, a sword, a revolver and belt, my watch and a few rupees on the chair by my bedside, and a host of smaller articles were gone, worst of all my beloved gun and its case.

The whole thing flashed upon me; the "Oochlias" had paid me a visit! The lad had been sent through the camp on purpose to raise an alarm and draw us all away from my tent, but incautiously going too near had been boned by "Tim." Meantime his confederates had quietly gutted my tent and decamped with the spoil. I don't think I ever felt so small—it was such a very transparent dodge. I comforted myself however, with the reflection that at any rate I should be able to find out in the morning to whom my prisoner belonged, but to my disgust, my peon came with a chapfallen face at daylight to report that the lad had somehow or other got away. We went over to the "Oochlia" hamlet, of course, but no lad, it was stoutly declared, was missing from the families; no lad present bore the marks of "Tim's" teeth, none of my things were found in the village, nor was anything ever traced, except the gun-case, with my name on it, which was found some months afterwards in a dry watercourse several miles away.

How my plausible friends of the preceding evening must have chuckled over the whole business! I may mention that it is a very favourite dodge of these people to raise an alarm by fire or otherwise at one end of an encampment of travellers, while some of their party loot at the other end.

These gentry have gradually transferred their attention to the railways, and hardly a passenger train runs at night that does not carry some of them. They mingle with the people in the waiting sheds, very soon find out what bundles are worth annexing, and where the owners are going, then take tickets themselves for some nearer station, and travelling in the same compartment, either watch their opportunity for making off with the bundles during the night, or drop them out of the window near the station they themselves are to alight at, whence they walk down the line till they find the spoil. Of course there are hundreds of other opportunities afforded to them during a long journey and in crowded compartments, of practising their profession. Every new section of railway opened extends the field for their operations.

The Railway Police are fully cognisant of what goes on, and they do their utmost to warn third-class passengers against "Bamptias," but I fear they are not as yet very successful in catching any of the rogues. It is the old story—there are no detectives.

CHAPTER XVIII.

CRIME DURING THE FAMINE.

FEW men who witnessed the last Deccan famine (1877-79), fewer still of those whose lot it was to be employed officially in coping with it care to talk much about their dreary experiences, but those ghastly years are burnt into their memories nevertheless, and can never be forgotten to their dying day.

Who *can* ever forget that brazen sky overhead, that hideous brown-black landscape destitute of vegetation, parched and cracked by the sun's fierce heat, swept almost throughout the night and all the day long by sand-laden blasts hot as from a fiery furnace? Who can forget the miserable cattle, mere hides stretched over skeletons wandering or rather staggering about in vain search for food and water and lying dead or dying along every roadside? Who can forget the living human skeletons dragging themselves to the nearest relief work or hiding in their desolated homes to die, whole families together, of starvation? Day after day, week after week, month after month, for two whole years hardly a cloud in the sky, hardly a drop of rain, the riverbeds dried or drying up—cholera raging everywhere!

It so happened that I saw some weeks of the Bengal famine in 1873-74 while on a visit during privilege leave to a relative, a planter in Behar. I can honestly say that I never witnessed all that time, nor did I hear tell of such misery as was to be seen any day in the "arid zone" of the Deccan in the first year of that famine before relief measures had been well inaugurated. I believe the difficulties of grain transport and distribution were much greater in the Deccan than they ever were in Behar, certainly large districts blessed with a superabundance of food grains were nearer to the famine-affected area in Behar. Money, too, there was comparatively plentiful and the State poured out treasure with a lavish hand, regardless of expense. In the Deccan, on the other hand, the calamity had to be dealt with almost parsimoniously, for strict economy was the order of the day.

I am not going to discuss who was right or who was wrong on various questions of famine management. Are not these vexed points laboriously discussed in the various official papers which culminated in the admirable Famine Code which only two years ago was found to work so well? With the country now traversed by good roads and covered by a network of cheap railways the calamity of 1877-79 ought never to occur again, even in the "arid zone," for the administration now really has for the first time its finger on the pulse of the country, never again will matters be allowed to drift in the hope that they will somehow mend, never again will the railways be found insufficiently supplied with rolling-stock and engines, never again will the Government lack a complete scheme of relief works for every district. There may be scarcity, but there never ought to be a famine again.

Thinking back now over the criminal statistics of the decade ending in 1880, it is easy to perceive the growth of some forms of crime, the disappearance of others, as distress began to be felt, as it became more and more acute, as it afterwards died away. A highly interesting not to say instructive, diagram might, I am sure, be prepared from the criminal returns for the years 1875 to 1880, and I deeply regret now that I did not bring home with me the reports that would be necessary for its preparation. As it is, I can only write from memory, aided by notes and diaries of a not very comprehensive kind.

With the first sign of bad season, with the rise in prices of all food grains, dacoity, which had been at the lowest ebb ever known began steadily to increase. By dacoity I do not mean the mere robbery without violence of grain by half-a-dozen half-starved wretches, which, under the Penal Code, has to be classed as "dacoity," but I mean the real old-fashioned dangerous dacoity by desperate characters armed in some way with bill-hooks, clubs, and an occasional sword, whose victims were not necessarily a petty grain merchant, but more commonly wealthy Sowkars and Marwarris (money-lenders).

Organisation soon became observable in these crimes. Leaders came to the front, the Nizam's frontier again became disturbed, well-armed bands, occasionally mounted, crossed over the frontier to commit outrages in quite the old style. In a district where a dozen dacoities of the mild Penal Code type had lately been regarded as a heavy record for a year, there began to be two or three real dacoities in the month, and the number rapidly increased until almost every post that came brought a report of a dacoity of one sort or another.

Strange that at such a time, when hundreds of desperate and reckless men infested the country, not a single attempt was made—at least, in my recollection—to rob the mail-carts, though it was a matter of common knowledge that millions of rupees worth of ornaments and other valuables were being daily sent up in them to be melted down and converted into coin of the realm. In the famine years there can be no doubt, for instance, that the mail contractors of the long postal line from Dharwar *viâ* Belgaum, Kolhapoor, and Satara to Poona, safely conveyed property of this kind to the value of several crores of rupees. What special precautions were adopted by the contractors I am not aware, but the fact remains that they cheerfully undertook this tremendous responsibility and acquitted themselves splendidly of their dangerous duty.

What good fellows, by the way, are the Cursetjees and Nowrojees, the Cowasjees and Pestonjees, engaged in these enterprises! How many poor ladies and children could never get away to the Hills, but for the liberal credit generously extended to them by the Parsee phaeton and tongawallas! How much they have lost by their generous forbearance is known only to themselves and never spoken of by them.

Well, we led the dacoits all over the country a terrible life of it. What with stirring up the Nizam's Government to exert something like authority along the frontier, what with numerous additional police posts and incessant patrolling by sowars (mounted police), hundreds were caught and convicted on our side of the boundary line, and hundreds more escaped into the Mogulai or Nizam's territory, where there is very little doubt not a few were quietly shot or hanged out of the way.

Meantime, relief works of sufficient magnitude capable of employing any amount and every description of labour having been set fairly going, hundreds of restless spirits abandoned depredation and settled down quietly on the works. Serious dacoities then began to diminish as rapidly as they had sprung up, and we soon had little crime to contend with (*at a distance from the railway line*), beyond small thefts and robberies of grain. Of these, of course, there were thousands every month to the overflowing of every gaol and subordinate gaol.

On the whole, however, considering the deplorable condition to which the people were reduced there was much less thieving than I should have expected, the poor creatures were wonderfully patient, wonderfully good to each other while the charity of the well-to-do knew no stint.

I have above italicised the words "*at a distance from the railway line*," because the exigencies of the famine requiring the transport by day and night of thousands of tons of food-stuffs by railway, gave birth to wholesale depredation of quite a novel character on the Great Indian Peninsular lines. Heretofore a loaded train of open trucks was always perfectly safe from theft as it passed up or down-country, grain bags here and there might be opened in the goods yards and some of the contents pilfered, but such a thing as the carrying off of whole bags at a time was unknown.

Now all was changed. Heavy trains compelled to travel slowly up certain "banks" or steep inclines were boarded as they went along by bands of men who threw the bags down on the embankment by dozens where their confederates loaded them into carts or on pack-bullocks and ponies and drove away. The guards one or two perhaps to one train, were powerless, of course, and more often than not on dark nights were utterly ignorant of what had been going on, or they were driven by showers of stones to remain under the cover of their guards' boxes.

On the arrival of the train at its destination, trucks were often found half emptied. The consignees lodged a claim against the Railway Company for the loss, the Company paid up freely, and the game went merrily on. The perfect impunity with which these robberies were effected, the facility with

ROBBERY OF OVERLADEN GRAIN TRAINS DURING THE FAMINE.

[*To face p.* 193.

which the stolen goods could be got rid of, attracted all the daring spirits in the country side. Bheels, Ramoshis, Kolees, and Ryots worked together with a will and the petty grain-dealers everywhere egged them on and acted as receivers.

I rarely succeeded in tracing through my police any of the bags thus stolen. Empty sacks were found in abundance, now and again petty dealers were found in possession of grain that could not have been honestly come by, but of evidence there was little or none obtainable. The villagers for miles on each side of the line, from the Patels or headmen, downwards, were banded together and doubtless shared in the gains. One might have had some sympathy if they had been starving villagers seeing vast quantities of the grain they needed to support life slowly passing their doors unguarded. But these were by no means starving people. The spots at which trains were thus looted were not even within the famine limit, and though prices of grain, no doubt, ruled high in consequence of the neighbouring famine, the people near the inclines were not in want. On the contrary, they were remarkably well-to-do, for even the Bheels, the Ramoshis, and the Kolees in the vicinity had not seriously felt the pinch of famine. Thousands upon thousands of bags of grain of all sorts, worth several lakhs of rupees, were thus made away with.

Long after it was all over I obtained some insight into the organisation. It was the grain-dealers, of course, who instigated the robberies. They paid from

Rs. 2½ to Rs. 5 a bag to the villagers, according to what its contents were, whether "jowaree," "bajree" wheat, or "dal." They had storage room and grain pits in which to store the contents with their own grain. They refused to keep the sacks which were burnt or torn up and scattered about the fields.

The organisers of the raids were the village Patels and a few naiks or chiefs of the Bheels and Kolis. The carts, bullocks and pack-animals belonged to the Patels and villagers. The actual robbers who mounted the trains were villagers, Bheels and others, employed and paid for their trouble at so much per bag brought away. They became very daring and expert in boarding moving trains, but several of them lost their lives in jumping off. I remember one poor wretch found with his head severed from the trunk, and another with both his legs cut off was found still alive in the morning. A very rich harvest was doubtless thus earned during eighteen months or more by the inhabitants of villages near these "banks."

But the evil by no means stopped there. Gate-keepers can easily cause a train to be pulled at night for five, ten, or twenty minutes by displaying a light, on the excuse that they heard something on the line. Signalmen can delay signals, and what so simple as to have their "pals" in readiness to board a train thus pulled up? Yard watchmen, too, had their "pals," and gradually most of the subordinate rank and file employed on the railway yielded to temptation.

Lastly, shrewd heads were laid together, "Bunias"

(merchants) conferred with native station-masters, and the game of false consignments began. For thirty or forty bags actually loaded in a truck the station-master would sign for fifty or sixty, the difference being ultimately paid for by the Company and the loss attributed to theft by the Bheels in transit. There were dozens of other ways in which the Company were similarly defrauded; the curious will find them set out in the Report of the Commission which at last was nominated to inquire into these robberies and to devise means for stopping them—it was a document which attracted considerable attention in 1879–80.

I am not going to take the side of either of the parties to the controversy that followed. In my humble judgment both parties were partly wrong and partly right. The two Government members of the Commission distinctly under-estimated the depredations by the villagers of which I have given but a faint description above. They ran away too much at the start with the idea that the railway subordinates were principally responsible for the losses, and deeply implicated in the frauds. The railway nominee, on the other hand, could not bring himself to believe that his people could have been guilty—every one must sympathise with him—nor would he see that there had been shortcomings in the matter of supervision.

Such shortcomings were inevitable under the pressure of a sudden and extraordinary traffic for which the Company, through no fault of its own, was

o

unprepared. The Government, whether of India or of Bombay I will not presume to say, was mainly responsible for that unpreparedness. Had they not refused or delayed sanction for the large addition to the engine strength and rolling-stock previously demanded by the Company, the railway yards would not have been blocked, overladen trains need not have been despatched to crawl up steep inclines, or, as often happened, to be taken up in sections. Then, again, the question of the Railway Police had been allowed to drift unsettled, till the force, always numerically insufficient, was more or less demoralised and worse than useless. There was a conflict of opinion too, as to the responsibilities and even as to the relative duties of District and Railway Police.

In these later days matters could not possibly gain such head. The railway is well provided with rolling-stock and has established a simple but fairly efficient system of checking, the Railway Police are as good as any police in the Presidency of Bombay, their relations with the District Police are cordial and their respective responsibilities are well defined. At the first recurrence of train looting at "banks" or elsewhere, reasons would be found for establishing punitive police posts in peccant villages near the scene of the crime, and there is nothing better calculated than a punitive post to break up these little village combinations! Nothing is more improbable than that the G. I. P. Railway will ever again have to disburse from ten to twelve lakhs of rupees by way of compensation for this sort of loss.

CHAPTER XIX.

DISARMING.

AMONG the string of penal laws which were enacted in rapid succession after the outbreak of the great Mutiny, or Sepoy Rebellion, of 1857 was of necessity the Disarming Act. Most district officers of the Western Presidency held a very decided opinion that it ought to have been applied much sooner. Be that as it may, I do not hesitate to say that this disarming was one of the most unpalatable duties that ever fell to my lot.

The gradual nature of the rise of British power in and around the territories conquered from the Peishwa—the year by year absorption into the British Army of the best fighting men in the Maratha Country, the Carnatic, and Guzerat—had till then precluded the idea of a general disarmament. It was our cue to pacify the country and the best way to do that was to gather under our colours all restless and turbulent spirits, to conciliate all petty chiefs and the heads of the village communities enlisting their aid and influence in the enforcement of order and the dispersal of the numerous gangs of armed robbers by which the country was infested.

It was necessary that the people should be armed for self-protection. Up to comparatively recent times the ryot, or cultivator, took his "talwar" (sword) and his matchlock into his fields as a matter of common precaution. As the country settled down, and our police organisation began to produce good results—so that cases of marauding and dacoity became few and far between—the ryot still continued for dignity's sake to take his arms with him to his field-work. It was the right thing to do. Not to carry arms was to show himself a mean mortal.

Gradually, however, the long cumbersome matchlock with its dangling paraphernalia for carrying powder and ball was left at home, and the "talwar" (sword) only taken out to work with, perhaps, a dagger or two in the waistband. Next, the "talwar" was hung up at home and the dagger only worn. But though no longer actually in use, the weapons were usually highly prized, kept in fair condition and always in requisition at any village festival. There were no restrictions whatever on the sale and purchase of arms or ammunition of any kind, every considerable village contained a skilled armourer or two, and some family who lived by manufacturing gunpowder.

When, therefore, the terrible tidings came from Meerut and Delhi, the Western Presidency, in common with the rest of India, was full of weapons of all kinds, offensive and defensive, from the common "Bichu," or scorpion dagger to the light "Jingal," or cannon on the village walls.

The first step enjoined by the Disarming Act was the registration of all arms of whatever kind. Every man from the highest to the lowest was required within a stated time to produce his weapons at the nearest Government office, where they were duly registered against his name, labelled, and stored away till such time as the Magistrate, Assistant Magistrate, or other duly-empowered official should decide whether he should be licensed to retain any arms at all, and, if so, which of them; or, if the owner so elected, they were broken up into small pieces and returned to him. Non-registration of arms or concealment of them was, if my memory serves me aright, punishable by fine and imprisonment, with or without hard labour, for six months. The fullest powers were given to Magisterial and Police authorities to search for arms.

I was at that time serving in the Ahmednugger District (or Zillah, as it was termed in those days) and I well remember the thrill of dismay which went throughout the land when the needful proclamation was promulgated. For some days it seemed as if the people could not believe that the Sirkar meant to carry out its stern resolve. Very few weapons were registered for a long time and those mainly by the sycophants around the Government offices. Cringing Brahmins, sneaking Kulkarnis (village accountants), were, of course, foremost not only to register such arms as their households held, but to pay off old scores by giving secret information of weapons owned by the Patels, or village head men, or any other individual against whom they happened to have a grudge. It needed a few examples, however, before the old Maratha Patels and farmers would register freely, and their reluctance, of course, did them harm when the question of their retaining arms was considered.

It was a pitiful sight to see a grand old Maratha Patel bring up the weapons of his family—many of these were heirlooms, as it were—matchlocks of cunning workmanship ornamented profusely with silver plates and wire—swords in richly-embroidered velvet scabbards—blades wrought of the finest steel, with handles curiously inlaid with gold and silver, or occasionally encrusted with rough jewels—daggers of fantastic design, similarly embossed—pikes, and spears, and maces. Most of them had histories, and were prized by their owners as the apples of their eyes. I am glad to remember that the Act was, on the whole, very humanely and considerately worked, though every day's post brought us down the news of some fresh horror in the north-west, and we knew not when the flame of insurrection might burst out in our very midst. The majority of the better class of weapons, such as I have described, were broken up by a blacksmith on the spot, and the pieces returned to the owners. Many a fine old fellow did I see receive his fractured favourites and go away with tears rolling down his cheeks. Many another— always a younger man—departed with a scowl of hatred on his visage, and doubtless the deadliest thoughts in his heart. But the thing *had* to be

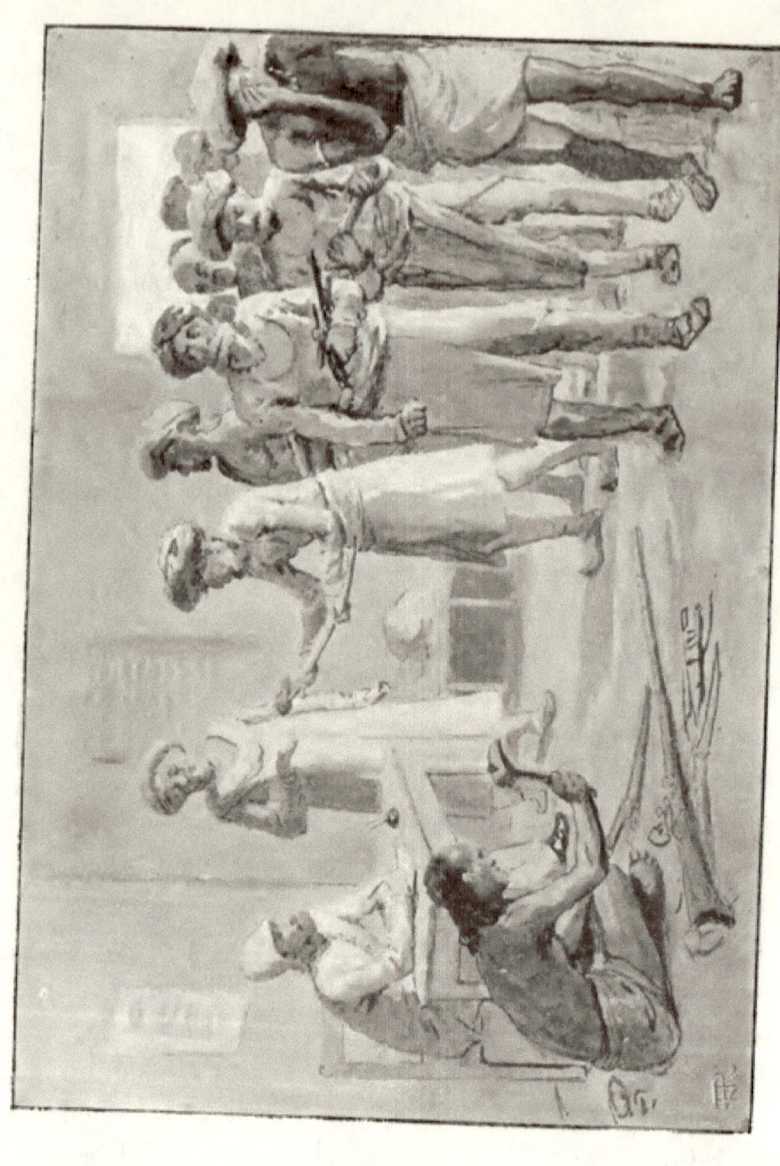

DISARMING. [*To face p.* 198.

done. It was "nasib," "kismet"—our fate and theirs.

Disarming the rural population, as I have above attempted to describe, though slow, was a comparatively easy task. It was when the larger towns' returns were scrutinised that the authorities perceived the great difficulties to be overcome. Large walled towns, with from ten to twenty or thirty thousand inhabitants, many of them the scum of the population—towns in which thousands of stands of arms were known to exist—registered only hundreds, and there was infinite difficulty in obtaining information, and great facilities for concealment. People living in towns, all the world over, know less of and care less for the affairs of their neighbours than the simpler residents of the country. The wily Brahmin of the town was quite as ready to betray his neighbour, of course, but then he had not much knowledge of his neighbour's inner life. Moreover, at that time, in every town of any importance there were emissaries from the rebels in the north inculcating caution and patience and holding out large promises to the riff-raff and scoundrels of rich "loot" when the "good time" should come. Our police had hardly been really reorganised for four years—were drawn from the most ignorant classes, and contained but little of the detective element. It was only by a very rigorous use of the powers of search and by making examples of the richer householders who had concealed weapons that any way was made. It is very doubtful if any large town was thoroughly disarmed.

It was at this time, during what was called the Bheel Rebellion—of which I shall have much to say hereafter—that I happened to be on the way from Kopergaum with a small force under Major Montgomery to attack the Bheels reported to be strongly posted in large numbers, under some notable "naiks," or chiefs, on the border of Khandeish. Perhaps it was fortunate for myself that I was recalled by an "express" from the Magistrate, for the so-called "battle of Mandwe" which followed was somewhat a bloody business for the force. My "express" directed me to proceed across country with all possible speed to Sangamnair, a small partially-walled town about eighty miles distant, where I should find sealed orders awaiting me in the hands of the officer commanding two companies of a native regiment then posted at the place. Now, Sangamnair was a place of evil reputation in those days, though I believe it is now controlled by an excellent Municipality and contains many enthusiastic adherents of the "National Congress." I can hardly accord higher praise to it surely than this!

It was known that a secret meeting had been held near Sangamnair between the Bheel and Koli leaders and an agent of Tantia Topee, at which the Bheel rising under Bhagoji Naik was decided upon, it was also more than suspected that seditious assemblages took place in the town. As a matter of course, I started at once, and, travelling with all possible speed, reached the Assistant Collector's bungalow the following afternoon.

Captain Simon—as I shall call him—handed me my sealed orders which informed me that I should in all probability receive a visit from a Madrassee military pensioner who had conveyed an offer to the Magistrate to give information as to where large quantities of arms of all kinds were concealed. I was to try to prevent the informer's identity being suspected,—was armed with the fullest powers of search and arrest and directed, moreover, personally to prosecute any individuals apprehended before the nearest European Magistrate. I may mention that scarcely one hundred miscellaneous and mostly worthless weapons had been registered, though it was notorious that the town was full of arms.

By eleven o'clock at night we had given up all hope of seeing our Madrassee friend and I had just turned into bed when I heard my faithful Portuguese "boy" saying, "Saheb! Saheb!" in that peculiar tone we know so well. Simon was roused, and in due course a muffled figure was ushered into a room, over the window of which we had taken the precaution of nailing a blanket. Our visitor was a fine specimen of the Madrassee low-caste sepoy, and had a slight limp from a wound received in Burmah. I shall neither name him nor mention his occupation, because his descendants are (or were, six years ago) still in Sangamnair. There was no humbug about him, at any rate, and he did not waste time. He gave me at once a list of the principal citizens in a certain street with a list of the weapons which he believed were hidden in their houses, adding a supplementary list of other houses he suspected but was not quite sure about. He also gave me valuable information, which was afterwards utilised, of nocturnal meetings convened in various houses. He asked for no reward; he was in no sense of the word, as ordinarily used, an "informer," but he was genuinely indignant at the "Nimmak-harams," or "faithless to their salt," who hung back from helping the "Sirkar." We, or rather I, saw him on several occasions afterwards. I am glad to say that, quite unsolicited by himself, he was well rewarded for other important intelligence, which always proved reliable.

My friend Captain Simon was no idler and had not passed a solitary three months at Sangamnair with "pegs" and cheroots. He had made an excellent topographical survey of the country round and a fair plan of the town itself, with every street and lane of which he was familiar. Before we finally turned in we had studied these documents and decided on our next morning's campaign. The *reveillé* was sounded at four o'clock, eighty men told off under arms; having fortified our inner men with eggs and bacon and strong coffee, Simon and I marched off at the head of them to the ferry which crossed the Sangam, or junction of rivers. By daylight we held every approach to the particular street named by our Madrassee friend, and sentries were posted to prevent the egress or ingress of any person. The surprise was complete; we took house by house in turn and ransacked it, "inside, outside, and in my lady's chamber." Many a wrinkle I got that morning of the way to search a native house! Many a queerly-devised treasury and place of concealment did I see! Many weapons were found in these secret places, including numerous British-made pistols, but it was on the flat roofs that we made our greatest hauls. There, as is common in many Deccan towns, were stacked the "kirbee" or "jowari" stalks—the cattle-fodder of the country—great piles of unthreshed bajri (millet) and of the mal-odorous cow-dung cakes, or "brattles" (as some English writer terms them), the fuel of the country. In and under these heaps, which we ruthlessly pulled to pieces, despite the owner's lamentations, we found any amount of matchlocks, swords and spears, and not a little powder in bags. I remember that on one roof we bagged twenty-five matchlocks and three good old "brown Bess" muskets: the curious thing was, all the weapons were in such good order—the matchlocks clean and bright and oiled—the swords as sharp as razors! In the six selected houses, inhabited by one Brahmin, a Purdèsi, three Mahomedans, and two Marathas, we found over three hundred weapons, with which stacked in carts and our six prisoners we returned blithely enough to a late breakfast.

I arranged to take my prisoners off next day to Mr. Chapman's Camp, forty miles distant, at Sinnur, where they were in due course each sentenced to the full penalty. But the most amusing part of the incident occurred that night and was reported to me just as I was leaving with the escort on the second morning. The streets of Sangamnair were found bestrewn with every description of weapon, from the modest dagger to the old-fashioned double-barrelled gun! It was too late to register, and the panic-stricken owners had thrown or deposited them in the streets during the previous night. Thus was Sangamnair disarmed!

I have often thought what a subject this would have been for the pencil of Gustave Doré—the waning moon—the narrow streets and rather lofty houses—the guilty owners stealing out to get rid of their illicit arms, or, maybe, to deposit them in the roadway opposite the house of an obnoxious neighbour.

NOCTURNAL DEPOSITS.

CHAPTER XX.

AGRARIAN CRIME.

"AGRARIAN murder," "agrarian outrage," the dictionary describes as "an outrage or a murder brought about by some dispute as to the occupancy of land." While Ireland has been earning for herself unenviable notoriety as the country beyond all others in which both these crimes are endemic, India, on the other hand, has a gradually diminishing record, although disputes as to the occupancy of land are common—especially in certain districts the South Konkan for example—where earth-hunger has always prevailed—every little plot of cultivable land is tenaciously held and the complexities of tenures tend to the multiplication of feuds, whether between superior and inferior holder or between the ordinary "Ryots" holding direct as tenants of the State. It may almost be said that, in the greater part of India, notably in the Western Presidency, agrarian outrage, in the sinister sense in which it is now journalistically used, is nearly unknown.

Stacks of grain or forage especially when standing out in the fields are frequently burnt, no doubt, but it is rare that incendiarism is traced, or even suspected. Cattle are now and again poisoned, but it is usually found to be the handiwork of the lowest castes—the Mhars and the Mhangs—seeking to make profit out of the skins which are their perquisites as village servants. I have rarely heard of cattle-stabbing, houghing, or otherwise mutilating, in all my thirty-five years'. experience. From this detestable form of agrarian outrage the average Indian rustic shrinks with horror.

On the other hand—there was a time before the Revenue Survey finally determined the boundaries of villages and of each man's holding—when free fights such as the Irish peasantry delight in, were common, and crowns were cracked in orthodox Irish fashion, but for some years past, the *causa belli* having been removed, peace has reigned on the boundaries.

"Boycotting" is a science practically unknown to our Aryan brethren, except in so far as it is practised in respect of caste disputes and misdemeanours. No combination to boycott an individual by reason of a dispute as to the occupation of land has ever been brought to my notice. The simple "Ryot" is far behind the times, but there is no knowing how sapient he may become under the teaching of the far-famed "National Congress"—a body of unpretentious, unselfish patriots, of whom it is my anxious wish to speak with the humblest deference, seeing that they number among their leaders Members of Parliament—whom all the world recognise as most potential, sagacious, well-informed, disinterested, well-intentioned, well—anything you like in the way of praise that you can find in the biggest dictionary in the British Museum Reading Room!

On the other hand, again, "downright murder, brought about by some dispute as to the occupancy of land," is of comparatively common occurrence, though even that has notoriously diminished of late years. The march of education—the ever-increasing, and (I will add) improving breed of pleaders—the comparatively small cost of litigation under simple and excellent Civil Codes—have developed the native's innate love of litigation to its fullest extent. Besides, there is a prolongation of pleasure in worrying your adversary in the Law Courts, from month to month and year to year, with delicious little interludes in the shape of intrigues and cross-intrigues and occasional exchanges of virulent abuse. To knock your adversary on the head is but a transient—a very short-lived joy—apt, moreover, to lead to unpleasant personal results. So the field of battle now usually begins in the Subordinate Judge's modest chamber to be transferred in due course to the Judge Sahib's Court and ultimately to the sacred precincts of Her Majesty's High Court at the Presidency.

But occasionally one or other (or both) of the disputants becomes surfeited with the pleasures of litigation—hope deferred makes the heart sick. Evil counsellors among those interested in the never-ending suit and weary of it suggest more summary proceedings. Opportunities offer—a mere interchange of vituperation, especially if the dispute be among members of the same family, warms up into an assault, homicide or murder follows. Or the villagers holding under a middleman of the rack-renting type get sick of their lives and of him, he is attacked in his own house, or waylaid and done to death. But in any case of the latter description it may safely be presumed that the superior holder richly deserved his fate, he must have proved himself over many years, a curse and a scourge to the villagers and brought his fate upon himself.

I recall two cases of each of the types just described, which were noteworthy for other reasons. Before relating them I may mention that in the Southern Konkan the murder of the middlemen (or Khotes) was at one time very common. Feuds between them and the occupants possessing different proprietary, or quasi-proprietary, rights of occupation dated from before our Conquest in 1819 to 1822, were overlooked by the British Government for many years (deeply occupied as it was with the settlement of much larger and more important districts), and were much embittered and aggravated when the Government did take up the question in 1853, or thereabouts, by an ill-advised and ignorant attempt to fit a Deccani coat on a Konkani back. Flushed with the success that attended the Wingate Survey Settlement in the Deccan, where the "Ryot" holds direct under the Crown, well-meaning but locally inexperienced members of Council insisted on rigidly applying the same principles of settlement to the Konkan, where hereditary middlemen (Khotes) had existed for centuries, with privileged and unprivileged tenants under them. The result was, to say the least of it, disastrous and confusing, and, if I mistake not, three or four Khotes used to be knocked on the head every year in those troublous times.

But in all the cases that came under my notice, as, indeed, in every instance of agrarian murder " brought about by some dispute as to the occupancy of land," our Aryan brethren respected female life, and so far justified their title of the " gentle Hindu." In land disputes in India such an atrocity as shooting at, or in any way molesting, a woman has yet to be recorded. It has been reserved for "the foinest pisantry in the wurrld" to earn an infamous distinction for their ingenuity and persistent cruelty in harassing, maiming, and even murdering defenceless females.

But to get to my tales. In the immediate vicinity of Dapolie,* that charming little station so long the headquarters of the "Guttrams," or Native Veteran Battalion, is a little village—the name does not matter. It was held by a co-parcenary of Khotes or middlemen, of whom Mhadowrao, the youngest member of the family, was a *persona grata* to the European residents and district officials alike. He was in his turn holding the office of Police Patel when I first came to know him in the way of business, and a very efficient man I found him. Well, but not *too* well educated, he was an agreeable and entertaining

* Already mentioned in Chapter II.:—"*The Great Military Pension Frauds.*"

visitor and his manners were those of a high-born, high-bred Brahmin of the old school.

Time passed, and just as I was beginning to know my district and my men passably enough, I was (as a matter of course) transferred to act for a year or more in a higher grade in a distant district to revert ultimately to my substantive appointment. I took charge at Ratnagiri, and, as in duty bound, proceeded to inspect my Police Guards at the District Jail. I found there was a solitary convict in the condemned cells who was to be hanged for murder on the following morning. I went to inspect the cell, when, to my horror, I recognised through the bars my old friend Mhadowrao. *He* was not the least discomposed, but calmly told me that he was condemned to die for having beaten his old uncle to death in a dispute about some " Khote Khasgi," or private Khoti land, to which he and his uncle each laid claim.

It appears that his uncle and he, though bitterly hostile to each other anent this miserable plot of land, being members of an undivided family, occupied the same ancestral house actually living on different sides of it. One day, just before the midday meal, they met outside and a quarrel ensued, in the course of which Mhadowrao struck his old relative violently with a bamboo stick he had with him. The old man, endeavouring to save himself, shut himself into one of the outhouses, but Mhadowrao in his frenzy of passion burst down the door, belaboured him dreadfully about the head; finally, ferociously and atrociously mutilated the yet throbbing corpse. His fit of passion over, he calmly walked over to the Dapolie Police Station, gave himself up and volunteered a full confession.

The end of his life, however, was destined to be long remembered because of the mode in which he occupied his last few moments. I was at the execution as a matter of duty. Proceeding to the condemned cells, I found a native writer squatted outside the bars. Mhadowrao had asked for him to take down his last wishes while he calmly regaled himself on plantains and new milk. Naturally, I did not draw near till time was up, and then, ejaculating "*Arè* Narrayen! Narrayen!" at regular intervals, Mhadowrao walked composedly out and up to the drop and died instantly. So great was the feeling against the man that there were very few spectators, and it was with some difficulty that Brahmins could be found to superintend the cremation of the corpse.

I came to understand the feeling against him when I heard his last " will and testament " (so to speak) which he had been dictating up to the last moment. It was simply an injunction to his " Vakil," or pleader, to recover from some thirty or forty of his wretched tenants certain small specified measures of grain he claimed to be due from them!

The second case was a foul murder of a most estimable landlord by a clique of ruffians instigated by his enemies in the village. I have no hesitation in giving his name in full. Vithal Prabhu Desai, a high-caste Brahmin of a family resident at Harchèri, near Ratnagiri, for a century or so before the British Raj, succeeded to a lawsuit brought by his father against the British Government for illegal sequestration of his estates some fourteen years before. It was a very monster of a suit, the Jarndyce and Jarndyce of the Ratnagiri District Court. By 1859-60 there must have been few Judges and Assistant Judges in the Presidency who had not tried to unravel its skein of technicalities. To carry it on, so much as remained of the family estates was from time to time mortgaged: Vithal Prabhu was heavily indebted to the leading pleaders, and oft obliged to make his own motions in person. He practically lived in the Court, and had he not possessed many good friends, who honoured him for his well-known probity and believed in his wrongs, he might even have starved.

At last there came two Senior Assistant Judges in succession, who determined to clear the case off the file. The first decided most of the points in Vithal Prabhu's favour. Government and Vithal Prabhu both appealed to the High Court who returned the suit for fresh argument on certain issues, and then the Senior Assistant Judge (Baron Larpent) finally passed a judgment, which was upheld by the High Court. To a substantial extent Vithal Prabhu was restored to his ancestral possessions, and great was the satisfaction felt throughout the country side.

Restoring Vithal Prabhu, however, involved the ousting of certain parties who for years past had profited by his wrongs, and a fresh series of suits on minor points ensued, which I need not particularise. Suffice it to say that Vithal Prabhu was gradually carrying all before him. But he had naturally imbibed a taste for litigation, and, it may be, he was not altogether prudent or forbearing in his treatment of certain of the sub-tenants who had been, or still were, hostile to him. It followed that there was a strong party inimical to him in Harchèri.

About this time I was leaving the district for good, and Vithal Prabhu, between whom and myself there was a warm friendship, wrote to say he was coming in from Harchèri the next morning to say farewell. I was loitering about the station paying adieux to others in the early morning, when a procession met me near the Civil Hospital, carrying a body on a bier. It was the corpse of poor Vithal Prabhu Desai, grievously battered about the head and chest. He was leaving Harchèri at daybreak to come over to see me, when he was waylaid at a lonely spot by about a dozen men who literally beat the life out of him. It was little satisfaction to learn that some of the actual perpetrators were brought to justice, for if I remember aright, none of the instigators of the crime were ever successfully prosecuted.

CHAPTER XXI.

JAILS.

In the matter of Prison organisation and management there has been during the past thirty years an mprovement as steady as in most other Departments of the Administration. Indeed, the great and central prisons, Agra and Yerowda, for example, compare favourably with any jail in England. On the whole there has been less to correct in India where, as yet, happily, faddists have not had their way. Defective in structure, and often, from epidemics of particular forms of crime, or from the disturbed state of the country, jails were from time to time over-populated, sanitation was more or less neglected, discipline was apt to be lax, especially in the case of prisoners of the higher castes. But no such brutalities and infamies were perpetrated under the name of the Law as were exposed by Charles Reade in his well-known novel, ' 'Tis Never too Late to Mend.'

In the early " Fifties " the Straits Settlements sent their long-term convicts to Bombay where they were mostly drafted to moist and (to them) congenial climates, Tannah, Ratnagiri, and the like, and by good behaviour earned tickets-of-leave to the Hill Stations, Mahabuleshwar and Matheran, and became the market-gardeners, shoemakers, and what not of the place, many of them preferring to remain after their time was expired, respected and respectable citizens often possessed of considerable wealth.

About this time the Ratnagiri Jail, capable of containing about three hundred and sixty convicts, was choke-full; at least two-thirds were Chinamen and Malays from the Straits—ruffians, each with a record of piracy or murder, or both combined. Many of them were heavily fettered and carefully guarded by armed Police when at their ordinary work in the "laterite" quarries, for they were mostly powerful men; the tools they used were formidable in their hands—there were known to be deadly feuds among themselves that might break out at any moment. Nevertheless, the punishment sheet was marvellously clear, breaches of jail discipline were much fewer among these desperadoes than among the milder Hindoos in the work-sheds within the jail. The fact in due time penetrated the intelligence of the powers that were at Bombay Castle, inquiries were instituted as to why pirates and murderers, usually very obstreperous in other places, should become so tame at Ratnagiri, but the riddle had yet to be solved.

For some years one Sheik Kassam had been the jailor. Belonging to the fisherman class and possessed of very little education he had, nevertheless, worked his way upwards through the Police by dint of honesty, hard work, and a certain shrewdness which had more than once brought him to the front. At last, towards the end of his service the jailorship falling vacant, he was, with every one's cordial approval, nominated to the post. With comparative rest and improved pay the old gentleman waxed fat,

THE MODEL JAILOR.

and a jollier-looking old fellow, or withal a more genial companion, the country round could not produce. The cares of State, the responsibility of three hundred murderous convicts weighed little on Sheik Kassam.

He developed, as was afterwards remembered, a remarkable talent or predilection for gardening, almost from first taking office; he laid out the quarry-beds, brought water down to irrigate them, produced all the jail required in the way of green stuff, and made tapioca and arrowroot by the ton. The better plot of land belonging to the jail lay between Sheik Kassam's own official residence, a tiny "bungalow"-fashioned dwelling with a walled courtyard, near to the high road. The Sheik had no difficulty in obtaining permission to erect a high wall of rubble from the quarries along the whole road frontage, so that—as he urged—the convicts at work in the garden would not be gazed at by passers-by, and that forbidden articles, such as tobacco, sweetmeats, liquor, and the like, should not be passed or even thrown over to them.

In due course this favourite slice of garden was safely boxed in from the public view by a wall some eight feet high, extending from the jail itself round to the jailor's house, the only entrance to it being a little wicket-gate by the side of the Sheik's backyard.

Time went on, when some envious or malicious Brahmin desirous of currying favour with the Doctor Saheb, or whoever the Superintendent was, revealed to his amazed ears that Sheik Kassam's disciplinary system consisted in his having the most dangerous of the Chinamen and Malays quietly into his backyard from the garden, and there regaling them with plenty of sweetmeats, sugar, moderate potations, aye even with female society of a peculiar sort! If Chingfoo or À-chin became unruly or saucy he could, and sometimes did, get a dozen lashes; but if these worthies behaved decently, they had their little festival in due rotation. Poor old Sheik Kassam's character as a model jailor was gone, of course; he was dismissed, but I am glad to say with a full pension, which he did not live long to enjoy. He never could be brought to see that he had done anything wrong!

Running "Amôk."

Sheik Kassam was succeeded by a stalwart young Eurasian possessed of unusual courage and resolution, the punishment book filled up and the "cat-o'-nine-tails" was in constant requisition for a time, till the worst of the convicts found that they had a man over them not to be trifled with yet never vindictive or unjust. It was during this man's incumbency that a remarkable instance occurred of the feuds which, I have above observed, are, or rather were, so common among the Straits Settlement convicts. Chang-Sing was a powerful, rather tall Chinaman from Singapore, with a good-humoured grin on his face, not half a bad fellow by any means, whose name never figured in the black book. He was a life-convict for piracy and murder. So, too, was Buddoo, a Malay, a sort of human scorpion in appearance—short, with enormously broad shoulders, bow-legged, and with a malignant scowl on him that would "sour butter-milk," as they say in Ireland. He, too, came from Singapore, and it was no doubt during some of their joint "divilries" that Buddoo's hatred of Chang-Sing was engendered. The former came to Ratnagiri with the character of the most dangerous, incorrigible convict in the gang. No punishment deterred him, his fiendish cruelty knew no bounds; he would upset scalding water at the cooking-place over the back of an unoffending fellow-prisoner, he would drop a live coal on the man working with him at the forge, he would run sharpened bamboos into any one near him, and the more you flogged him or locked him up in the solitary cells, the more he grinned and did not care.

His intense animosity to Chang-Sing being known, they were never allowed to meet, except at general parades. Chang-Sing was mostly in the quarries. Buddoo worked in the interior of the prison at shoe-making and other leather work at which he was very expert.

The Ratnagiri Jail, designed by Major Outram, brother of the great Sir James, whose lamentable fate need not be here referred to, is peculiarly adapted for the separation of the convicts. Stone arched passages, secured by strong gates, lead from one working yard to the other, from one dormitory to the other; but there is a common stone staircase leading up from the entrance yard to the dispensary and hospital. Chang-Sing received some contusion or injury in the quarries, and was on the sick list. Buddoo must have heard of it, he ran the point of an awl into his own finger, and with this excuse was permitted to go to the dispensary at a time in the morning when he knew he would be tolerably sure of seeing Chang-Sing upstairs or somewhere. He secreted himself in an angle on the stairs, having in each hand a shoemaker's knife. Chang-Sing was coming up the steps, when Buddoo jumping on him, struck him downwards two frightful blows, one of which severed the jugular vein, while the other penetrated the lung. Brandishing his weapons and covered with blood, Buddoo made off down the passage to his working shed; but the alarm had been given, the gate was closed, and a convict warder barred his way. Him Buddoo wounded in half-a-dozen places, while the poor fellow was opening the lock. With fiendish yells and howls—the other convicts flying before him—he made for his own working corner and squatted down.

The guard promptly enough surrounded him with bayonets fixed; even then, Buddoo, springing suddenly forward, plunged one of his knives into a Sepoy's arm. At this moment the Police Superintendent, a cool, calm Scot (who subsequently rose to high office in other colonies), appeared on the scene, and hit upon the following ingenious device for taking the miscreant alive.

Buddoo was crouched in a corner of a large, open work-shed with a low, four-foot mud wall all round it by way of protection from the weather. Our canny Scot obtained a stout fishing-net from the village and had it adroitly thrown over Buddoo from the outside, the police ran in, and Buddoo jumped up like a rabbit in a snare and was easily disarmed.

I happened (in virtue of another office I held at

CATCHING HIM ALIVE. [*To face p.* 221.

the time) to be the *ex-officio* Superintendent of the jail, but I was out for a morning ride, and only arrived just in time to see Buddoo locked up, Chang-Sing and the warder dead, while the policeman was lying bandaged up, and sweepers were mopping up the blood.

In my official report to the Inspector-General, while felicitating the canny Scot, I ventured to hint that, had I been present myself, I should probably have ordered the guard to load with ball, given Buddoo two or three minutes by my watch to throw his knives forward, and on his failing to do so, should have shot him like a rat.

I was gravely censured for the idea, but I think that even now, under similar circumstances, with a life-convict—a pirate and murderer from the first, who had just murdered two other men and wounded a third—I should certainly cheat the gibbet of its due rather than risk another life, or another wound to any one.

A Convict Joker.

A somewhat comic incident that occurred later at the same prison on the coast may be found amusing to my readers and a little refreshing also after the above sanguinary tale.

The Senior Assistant-Judge was again in official charge of the jail, a gentleman who died at Ratnagiri some years subsequently, beloved and regretted by all. The jail was about half full of the criminal population of the district, when some outbreak occurred among the Waghiris, a semi-barbarous tribe near distant and sacred Dwarka. Drafts of prisoners, made in the so-called insurrection were sent down to Ratnagiri, to the infinite disgust of the Civil Surgeon, who speedily found skin diseases of various loathsome forms appearing in his hitherto nearly empty Jail Hospital.

Towards the end of May, just before the monsoon closes the sea traffic, it moved the Government at Bombay to send down another draft of genuine Bombay jail-birds, with whom the House of Correction and the City Jail were inconveniently crowded. It was my duty to receive these gentry on their debarkation from a Shepherd's steamer, and to search them then and there. I may mention, without in any way intending to cast reflection on the Bombay Jail authorities, that there was scarcely a man who had not something contraband, such as tobacco or hemp decoction (Ganja) or opium, concealed somewhere about his person. One nimble youth had even three currency notes of rupees fifty each stowed away neatly under, or rather in, his armpits. They were a motley crew, indeed—the sweepings of a large city—burglars, common thieves and pickpockets, swindlers of all castes and classes, many of them with fifteen, eighteen—one, I remember, with twenty-two corrections standing to his credit. They did not contribute to the discipline of the jail, as may well be imagined.

However, weeks rolled on, and they shook down fairly well, for "Jupiter Pluvius" at Ratnagiri during the months of June and July is calculated to damp the most ardent spirit. But the skin diseases spread rapidly, and the Doctor, in despair, recommended that there should be weekly sea-bathing parades; this the Senior Assistant-Judge approved. There was a peculiarly suitable site for the purpose not far from the jail on the beach just below the Adawlat (the Judge's residence), where a tidal river flows out and meets the sea, forming an impassable bar throughout the Rainy Season. Accordingly, every Sunday morning the convicts were marched down in batches to the brink of the creek, where, surrounded by a strong cordon of armed Police, they were ordered to undress and bathe. Meantime, a boat conveyed half-a-dozen Police to the opposite shore, lest any adventurous spirit might swim over and try to escape. The whole scene lay in panoramic view from the verandah of the Senior Assistant-Judge's house above; and the residents of the station while taking "Chota Hazri," or early Sunday breakfast, with our friend, could watch all that went on, and, with binoculars, easily discern the features of the bathers below.

Most of the convicts, of course delighted in the swim and there were many very expert swimmers among them; but the Waghiris seemed to have a mortal aversion to cold water. It is said that the aboriginal black of Australia is the filthiest human being under the sun. Hottentots may run them close, no doubt, and the noble Red man of North America, as I smelt him years ago, must be bad to beat, but I would cheerfully back those Waghiris against them all! However, after being forced for several Sundays running into the water, they too became more approachable. The general health of the prison steadily improved; our worthy Civil Surgeon went about rubbing his hands, while the jail consumption of sulphur ointment went down to next to zero.

One lovely Sunday morning, during a break in the monsoon, the Civil Surgeon, myself, and two or three others were as usual up in the Adawlat verandah, when suddenly a violent commotion was visible among the bathers below—Policemen and bathers running over the sand towards the "surging bar." One of us fixing his binocular, exclaimed that a convict was being swept out to sea and was struggling in the surf. We all scampered down, except our host, who had to get something on besides his pyjamas; he was a wary man, and bethought him to take a thoroughly good look at the drowning man with his "Dollond" before he left the verandah to join us, which he did (to our surprise) very leisurely just as the supposed corpse was carried ashore by a couple of fishermen who risked their lives to recover it.

"Stand back, every one," said he, "the rascal is only shamming! I've been watching all his antics in the water. He was either playing the fool, or bent on trying to escape! Examine him, Doctor!"

A very few moments elapsed, when the Doctor rose up, laughing, and pronounced that the fellow (whose name, by the way, was Bindoo) was as well as any of us, and was shamming dead—he was not even exhausted!

"Get up, Bindoo," quoth the Judge. No movement. "Lift him up," said the Doctor. Down dropped the body, all anyhow!

"Bindoo, if you don't get up and walk back to jail, you will be flogged!" Bindoo never stirred, beyond giving vent to a few spasmodic gasps.

"Very well, Bindoo! I shall send for the triangles." A policeman was accordingly sent off to have the triangles and the "cat" brought down by a couple of convicts. All the time, while we were laughing and chatting and tipping the two fishermen, Bindoo never moved a limb, though it was easy enough to perceive his efforts not to show his breathing.

The little *cortège* with the triangles, and a stalwart warder "cat" in hand, in due course arrived, and the triangles were set up close to Bindoo.

"Now, Doctor," quoth our judicial friend, "be good enough to examine the man carefully, and tell me if he is in good health, and can bear a dozen lashes."

"Sound as a roach—would bear twenty, easy."

"Well, Bindoo," said the Judge in Maratta, "I'm going to tie you up and give you a dozen lashes if you don't get up this instant."

A slight squirm of Bindoo's body, his eyes opened slightly, and ejaculating, "Yih burra Zoolum hai!" (this is big bullying). Bindoo sullenly rose to his feet and shook himself, and after muttering occasionally that he would appeal to the "Burra Recorder Saheb" (the High Court Judges), he went off quietly to the jail, being made to take his turn now and again at carrying the triangles.

Poor Bindoo! He never saw the sea again till he had served out his sentence. We afterwards ascertained that the man—who could give points to any London professor of diving—was perhaps the most noted swimmer and diver on the coast. Opinions differed, but my own conviction is that he was simply having a lark and had no real intention of escaping.

CHAPTER XXII.

LOAFERS.

Part I.

Many of my observant readers will probably at some time or other in their up-country life have seen a crow in the course of his predatory wanderings, when he has discovered the craftily-hidden nest of some outlaying guinea-hen. With what ecstasy does he proceed to scratch an egg out into the open; with what vigour does he drive his pickaxe-like beak at the shell, fondly expecting that, like other eggs, he will pierce and break it, and be speedily devouring the luscious yolk therein! Dig! dig! Peck! peck! The smooth, hard brown shell, to his amazement, resists his beak, and the egg rolls a little way off. He tries another, and yet another, equally in vain. "The devil's in the eggs," quoth he, as he hops to one of them, and, steadying himself on one leg, tries to grasp the egg with the claw of the other, with a view to delivering a deadly dig at the apex. No go! The egg from its peculiar shape is not to be firmly grasped, and his beak is useless. Beside himself with rage, he tries to lift it, with a view to carrying it up on to some neighbouring branch, whence he proposes to drop it on the ground, and then! But either the egg is too

PUZZLED CROWS.

heavy for him, or he cannot grasp it firmly. In his despair—caw! caw! caw!—he summons to the spot all the crows in the vicinity, and they rake out that nest: they all try with beak and claw, but the "divil" an egg can they fracture. Meantime their clamour has attracted the attention of the cook-boy, the gardener, or the herd-boy, who, bethinking himself of a possible snake, hastens, stick in hand, to the spot and promptly pouches the whole setting.

Much as great a puzzle was, and perhaps still is, the dusty, dirty British loafer to the up-country policeman or to the village Patel. They do not know what on earth to do with him. The man had probably slouched in the village from nowhere in particular soon after the sun became hot, and had either betaken himself at once to the village rest-house, or to some out-lying, shady-looking shed, extending himself full length, with a log or his scanty bundle for a pillow. A mighty serviceable-looking shillelagh reposes beside him. The village curs bark at him—from a distance, *bien entendu.* The village children, leaving their dung pies half kneaded, peep in fearfully at him. Two or three women, carrying water-pots on their heads, pass by, glance at him, and hurry on, gathering the folds of their "saris"* over their faces, and muttering a few words of prayer for protection to their favourite deity. The trusty Mhar, or village watchman, soon hears of him, comes and looks, and makes off to report that a "Saheb" is lying asleep or drunk at such a place.

For none of these things does the loafer care one jot. He would call to the children to come and play with him, but he is too lazy, too hot, perhaps

* Woman's dress.

too tired; besides, he knows well that he must keep quiet, "lie low" for the present, and that it will all come right presently. Sure enough, the Police Patel of the village soon makes appearance accompanied by a shopkeeper or two and ever attended by the trusty Mhar. Loafer lazily lifts himself on his elbow, and then something like the following conversation ensues :—

"Saheb! Salaam," salutes the Patel.

"Slam! old chap!" says the loafer who always has a very fair smattering of the worst Hindoostani at his command.

"Does the Saheb want a guide?" ("Saheb Bhoomia mangta?") asks the Patel, whose first anxiety is to get the white man out of his village as speedily as possible.

"Nay, nay, old fellow, 'tag gya sône mangta' (tired, want to sleep)—'peechee jaega'" (will go afterwards).

"Bhòt atcha, Saheb, aur khooch mangta?" (Very well, Saheb, do you want anything else?)

"Here, Dekho, old man! I'm beastly hungry and thirsty, don't you see? ('Bhót bhookâ, Samja? Kooch bi do.') Give me something," slapping his stomach and opening his mouth significantly.

A little confabulation between the Patel and his companions, and the Patel says, "Atcha Saheb—ham bèch dega" (All right, Saheb, I'll send), and makes off while Loafer, sitting up, calls after him, " Right you are, old cock! only be a little 'jeldie'" (quick).

Loafer composes himself to sleep, cursing the flies

LOAFER MAKES HIMSELF AT HOME. [*To face p.* 230.

and creation generally, or if he has a little "baccy" he sits up and smokes, spitting around quite genially.

After a time the Mhar again appears, with a pot of milk, a goodly platter of chow-pattis (unleavened cakes), perhaps a hard-boiled egg or two, a bunch of plantains—possibly even with a small piece of native-grown tobacco. Loafer eats and drinks his fill, lazily amusing himself by throwing pieces of bread to the village dogs who crowd round to fight over the morsels. He then betakes himself to solid repose, and sleeps the sleep of the just till evening.

In the meantime the Patel has not been idle: a messenger has been sent over to the nearest Police Post with a letter reporting that "a 'sojer' (white soldier), 'not a Saheb,' had arrived in the village, they were afraid, and wanted a Sepoy to come— God knows what might happen!" The blue-coat preserver of the peace duly armed with his musket, probably turns up in the evening and proceeds to interrogate our Loafer.

"Where has the Saheb come from?"

"From Bombay."

"Where are you going?"

"To Nagpore, darn yer!"

"Is the Saheb in a 'Phalton' (Regiment), or does he belong to the big Railway?"

"Phalton be d——d; going to a 'jaga' (employment) at Nagpur."

"But, Saheb, this is not on the right road; Saheb

should have gone by train from Pimpalgaum" (mentioning the nearest railway station).

"Tell yer I won't! Shall go as I choose; I ain't done anything!"

"Very well, Saheb! I shall report to the Burra (Big) Saheb."

"All right! Report, and be d——d!"

Exit blue-coat—Loafer contemptuously expectorating and "darning" the "whole biling of peelers." Blue-coat advises the Patel to let Loafer have some more food at night and to give him a few bundles of straw to lie upon, but on no account to let him have any liquor. Blue-coat then presently pays a visit to the liquor shop and solemnly warns the owner of the pains and penalties he will incur by supplying the white man with anything to drink.

Loafer has a capital supper with perhaps some "currybhat" (curry and rice) provided by a charitable shopkeeper: he may or may not (usually he does not) try it on at the liquor shop: he has a splendid night, and by the time the village is astir he is well on his leisurely way to some other village. He does not make long marches, Loafer doesn't: six or seven miles is far enough for him, with many little halts while he admires the scenery, or finds himself interested in the field work going on around him. An ordinary irrigation well with its Persian wheel and ramp has fascination for him and at such spots he is pretty sure to get a few plantains to eat, or a stick of sugar-cane to chew. When the sugar-cane is crushing he is in clover, for it is *de rigueur* with the hospitable farmer then to give a plenteous drink of the fresh juice to all comers. At such times then he often passes a week or more in the neighbourhood of the Sugar Presses, supplied with abundant "Kirbee," or straw, to make a wigwam of by day and to sleep upon at night, always generously fed by the farmer and his people. At such times he has even been supposed—*mirabile dictu*—to make himself useful in some sort of easy, lazy way!—but these reports require confirmation!

As a rule Loafer never steals—rarely drinks anything stronger than milk or fresh toddy juice; he is never much more truculent in his manner than I have above depicted him. Commonly, he is a mild, good-tempered soul, behaving well to the people and usually a favourite with the children. If he finds his quarters comfortable and stops on he soon becomes friends with the village elders; his "pidgeon" Hindoostani suffices to make himself fairly comprehensible and he is absolutely insatiable with his questions. "Bhôt bât karta" (He talks an awful lot), said a Patel to me once. "He asks questions all day long. Is he going to be a missionary, or what is he, Saheb?"

The career of such a loafer as I have described was often a long one; many of them, to my knowledge, travelled over the greater part of India without a four-anna bit they could call their own, behaving decently and being right hospitably treated wherever they went. They did no harm to any one so the law did not much trouble about them. The villagers did not particularly object to them, *only* they were mighty glad to see the last of them, especially if they were sickly, for it would have been a terrible calamity if any white man died in the village precincts.

Truculent or drunken loafers, on the other hand, had not a very prolonged run, though even to them —principally, no doubt, from fear, but partly owing to the innate kindliness of our Aryan brethren—

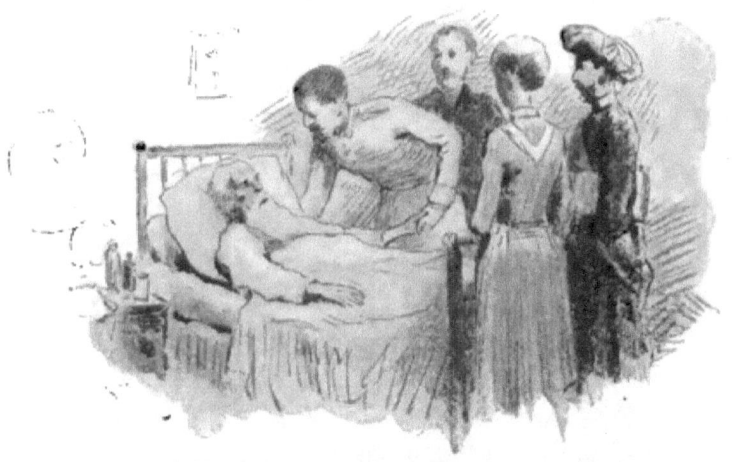

"THEY WOS VERY GOOD TO ME, THEY WOS."

unstinted hospitality was shown. These ruffians, who usually had a bad record, were soon followed up and "run in." In the end they naturally gravitated to the large cities and to the Presidency towns, where they were kept tolerably under control, as I shall hereafter relate.

Loafers, of course, have each his own history, which it is not difficult to trace. Occasionally, but rarely, it is a very pitiful one. Ordinarily, the record of the ruffian *is* that of a ruffian from start to finish; thief, or pickpocket, or village ne'er-do-well in his boyhood, he has enlisted, or gone to sea, has been discharged with ignominy, or run away; or has worked his way out to the "Injees" on the off-chance of getting employment on the Railways; or he has got employment and been kicked out; drink and dissipation in the large towns have ruined him, body and soul:—desperation finally drives him into the interior where he hopes for peace, and has heard that the "niggers" are very kind. "They wos very good to me, they wos," in the very words used by poor "Jo" of "Tom-all-alones,"* was almost the last sentence a poor dying wretch uttered to me once.

The record of the harmless, objectless, plausible loafer is, on the other hand, nearly always a simple record of the most incorrigible idleness. "Feckless" lads, they drifted rather than lived; their instincts, on the whole, were good and kept them from drink, riotous living, and dishonesty, mostly possessed of fair intelligence—some of them even cunning craftsmen, easily able to earn a good livelihood if they chose, but they never did choose—never overcame apathy—lived only for the day, caring nothing for what the morrow might bring. These, as they drifted aimlessly up-country, became imbued with Bohemian habits—they loved the open air, the freedom of their useless lives—caring nought, so long as they were not molested—well fed, they knew they always would be.

* See 'Bleak House,' by Charles Dickens.

Of both these types, with a large admixture of the criminal and semi-criminal classes, is mainly composed that vast army of the "Great unemployed"—the bane of the Home Secretary—the dread of London and every large city in Great Britain—at once the disgrace and the curse of their country.

On one memorable occasion, however, it was my lot to encounter a most mysterious loafer who belonged, so far as I have ever been able to ascertain, to neither of these types. It was in this way.

Just before the Pension Pay Frauds discovered by Colt, which I have related at the commencement of this series of papers, I rode out with Colt to a "Ghaut" road, or incline, which he was making about half-way between Dapoolie and Khèd. He was substituting a fairly practicable cart-road, with a gradient of about 1 ft. in 30 ft., for the zigzag bullock track that had existed for ages with a worn track about 1 in 10. There were two or three hundred men and women at work, and a good deal of drilling and blasting going on; so, while Colt descended to inspect, I too dismounted and seated on a comfortable boulder viewed the fair landscape below.

Suddenly I made out what was clearly a Briton's straw hat far below me, the wearer of it gradually hove in sight. It was a steep climb, so I had ample time to take stock of him as he paused now and again to mop his brows and to gaze over the valley through which he had just passed. He was a

THE MYSTERIOUS STRANGER. [*To face p.* 237.

red—healthy red—Englishman of about forty, very decently clad as to his understandings, carrying a white coat and a small bundle over his shoulders; in his right hand one of those long alpenstock-shaped canes peculiar to Kanara, the whole topped up by a stoutly-made and very broad-brimmed straw hat. He was above the average height and very powerfully built, with curly red-brown hair and large moustache, and a tremendous red beard flowing to his waist. A fine open countenance, but very resolute-looking mouth, completes the description of as fine a looking specimen of the British race as one would wish to see.

I knew every Englishman in the District, and, indeed, there was not one living within one hundred miles eastward of the place I sat upon; so, while he was toiling up the ascent I ran my mind over the descriptions of various deserters then wanted, but he was clearly not one of them. At last he topped the rise a few yards from me and very civilly doffed his straw hat, mopping his head while he bade me " Good morning, sir."

"Good morning," I said; "you've had a pretty stiff climb; sit down and rest a bit."

He complied, observing—

" Got a bit of baccy with you, sir ? "

I had, and in my holster also a big flask of cold tea, of which we partook together. Presently he said—

" 'Tain't much of a climb after those I've made beyond," pointing generally south and eastward.

"Ah!" quoth I, "you've had a longish tramp then! Where from, where to?"

"That's tellings," he replied, and seemed to become at once what North-countrymen call "main surly."

At this moment Colt reappeared, his inspection over. I tipped him a wink (to use a vulgarism)—he too sat down and we tried hard to pump our friend, but all in vain; he would only repeat, over and over again, that he was going his own way and wasn't going to be stopped by any one.

"All right, my friend," said Colt, "no one wants to stop you; but, you see, we are the Magistrate and Police Superintendent of the district and we've got to see that in these troublous times all Europeans are safe. Now, be the sensible man you are, and come along and put up a few miles hence with a grand old English Pensioner who has seen service, as I'm sure you have!"

"An old English Pensioner! that will I!" said the man. "Is't far from here, for I'm main faint?"

We told him it was only two miles off at the very side of the road he was travelling.

The grand old Pensioner was Daniel Monk, Pensioned Conductor of the Ordnance Department, the old recluse of whom I made mention in the second part of my Pensions' Fraud tale. We told our friend—who said his name was Johnson (good useful name, Johnson!)—that we would ride on and tell Monk to have breakfast ready, and that we ourselves hoped to see him later on. *Item:* we had friend Johnson carefully watched and followed at a distance by certain Mhars we could trust. He went, however, straight on, and was received at his gate by good old Monk who had a hot bath and breakfast ready for him. We called in the evening and were concerned to find that Johnson had a smart attack of ague, to which he said he was subject. This kept him at Monk's for some days. In the meantime I had ascertained from Mr. Forjett, the far-famed Commissioner of Police in Bombay, that he, Johnson, was not among the list of those "wanted" for desertion or anything else.

Monk had pumped him all he knew, but without much result. All he could tell us was that he was tattooed on the chest with an anchor and a heart and that he certainly had been with Peel's Naval Battery at Lucknow, that he was going to Bombay, and was intent on going the shortest road through Habsán, the territory of the Nawab of Jinjira, with whom the British Government was at that time at loggerheads, and where the crew of an English surveying vessel had just been stoned when landing for water.

Colt and I were decided that Johnson must not go by that route: Johnson was equally determined he would go that way and no other.

"Law, bless you," he said, "nobody will ill-treat me. Why, they've fed me well, and forwarded me on from village to village all the way from south of Cochin, right through the Portagee country (Goa), and wouldn't take an anna from me, though

I offered it! I've quite enough money, gentlemen, about me—let me have my own way, for God's sake!"

However, it was finally decided that Colt should take his passage to Bombay in a cabin "pattimar" (native vessel), such as usually worked in those days between Hurnee and Bombay.

Johnson came aboard all right and the vessel was to sail at early dawn, but after we left him Johnson persuaded the "Tindal," or native captain to put him ashore "for something he had forgotten." He never turned up again, and the ship sailed without him. Hurnee is a short eleven miles from Bankote at the boundary of the Habsán territory. Johnson walked over in the course of the night, persuaded the ferryman to ferry him over, and from that moment was lost to us.

The Political Department was set in motion to gain tidings of him, and it was found that he got up as far as Jinjira (the capital of Habsán), and there shipped on a native vessel bound for Bombay. Mr. Forjett subsequently ascertained for me that a man answering to his description had shipped as mate on some square-rigged craft bound for the Mauritius.

If Johnson be still alive and should by any chance read this little tale, he is earnestly requested to communicate with the writer, who is sincerely desirous of knowing his history and especially how he fared in the Habsán territory. He would not, I am sure, have taken ship there if he had found the people as hospitable as those farther south.

ZINJIBA (HABSÁN).

[To face p. 240.

UNIV. OF
CALIFORNIA

Johnson was of just the stuff to succeed in any of our colonies, and, maybe, he is now Blank Johnson, Esquire, a grey-headed Ex-Colonial Legislator and a millionaire, in which case I pray his pardon for making public this little page of his eventful history.

CHAPTER XXIII.

LOAFERS.

PART II.

It will, of course, be understood that my attempt to delineate a loafer's life in the preceding chapter related rather to old times—before his existence had forced itself on public notice, and it became absolutely necessary to tackle him seriously—in other words, legislatively.

It was about the beginning of the great speculation mania that set in in Bombay in 1862-63—a mania to which, I believe, if facts and figures were compared, the South Sea Scheme would sink into insignificance—that the loafer came to the front. How many are alive still to remember those silver times? When Reclamation schemes turned everybody's brain—when "Back Bays" fluctuated between twenty and forty-five thousand rupees premium—when "Mazagons" and "Colabas" followed suit—when there was a new Bank or a new "Financial" almost every day—when it was a common thing, in strolling from your office to the dear old Indian Navy Club, to stop a moment in the seething Share Market and ask your broker, "Well, Mr. B., or Bomanji! what's doing?" "Oh, sir! So-and-so Financials are rising —they say Premchund is buying." "Ah! well, just buy me fifty or a hundred shares" (as your inclination prompted you). You went to your "tiffin," or luncheon, at that memorable long table; you ordered a pint of champagne—no one ever drank anything but champagne in those days—you tried to get as near as possible to Doctor D. or poor T., the presiding geniuses of the meal, to obtain an "allotment" of a certain toast, which T. was justly celebrated for. Getting this, you were filled with exultation, for it was, and with reason, regarded as the precursor of other and more lucrative "allotments." Four o'clock saw you on your way back to office, and you stopped to ask your broker how your "financials" stood. "Rising slowly, sir!" would be the answer; with a calm conscience you said, "Then please sell mine," and the morrow brought you a cheque for fifty, a hundred, or two hundred rupees, as the case might be.

Why does not some abler pen than mine give an historical account of this great mania? When fortunes were made and lost in a few days; when the fatal telegram came announcing the peace between the North and South American States, and all our houses of cards came tumbling about our ears—when Back Bays (of which I was the happy possessor of *one*) rose to half a lakh premium— when "allotments" were sent to you "willy nilly," mostly worth some money—when poor Doctor D.

and Mr. T. were millionaires on paper! Many a pathetic story could be related of those times, and of the awful crisis afterwards; and of none could anything be more pathetic related than that of my old friend, Mr. T. I do not know if he is still in the land of the living. If he is, he will pardon me. *He* was no empty-bagged speculator, he had a handsome fortune when the mania set in, he had a lucrative appointment, which he gave up in his fatuous belief in the golden era which had dawned upon Bombay, and he was left by many a man whom he raised from poverty to affluence—how?

It was at this time, when the majority of citizens at Bombay were just as mad as the Ryots (cultivators) in the cotton districts, with their silver-tyred wheels, that Bombay, magnet-like, attracted "Loafer." From far and near they emigrated to Bombay as to an Eldorado. They infested the streets, they wandered about the suburbs, they became (the best of them) supervisors over the gangs of labourers on the Reclamation works. They offered their valuable services as occasional "gardeners" on Malabar Hill, and many thousands of beautiful rose trees and other shrubs did they destroy! Foolish people squandered money on them, as a natural consequence, "Loafer" became a public nuisance, and the newspapers of the day teemed with complaints about them. The quasi-philanthropists, the easy-going charitable people, shelled out rupees to them without any sort of inquiry. Loafer waxed fat; he took to drink, he became uproarious—occasionally he did a little business in frightening ladies left alone for the day, and at last he became an excrescence that could no longer be endured.

The Government of Sir Seymour Fitzgerald, compelled to take the matter up, convened a commission to "inquire and to recommend" in the usual flatulent parlance of a Government Resolution. The Chief Magistrate, Mr. Barton, was the President. Sir Frank Souter, the Commissioner of Police, and Mr. Gompertz, long connected with the Strangers' and Sailors' Homes, were two of the members. I will not attempt to describe the fun related of this Commission, partly because some of the Commission may be still alive, partly because I should be writing of matters of only local and temporary interest. In the result, a Vagrancy Act was drafted and adopted, and is now, so far as I am aware, the law which governs "Loafer." By it a Vagrant Ward was established in the Byculla Jail, and was very soon full of loafers of all sorts and kinds, very disgusted with themselves and humanity in general, and the curtailment of the liberty of the subject in their own persons. The Act also provided for the transmission of vagrants up-country to Bombay, and for their compulsory deportation under certain circumstances.

A few years after this occurred a most laughable incident of the up-country loafer. To relate it, I must go back some years. In 1857 or 1858, when

Lord Elphinstone was pushing every available white soldier to the front, there was a half regiment or so of the 33rd (Duke of Wellington's Own) retained at Poonah. It had to take the guard over the Civil Treasury, a place where there was always a goodly stock of rupees. One night, with these Europeans on guard, a very large sum of cash in bags disappeared. I believe it was six thousand rupees, in three bags of two thousand rupees each. There was not the faintest clue to the theft—nor has there ever been to this hour, though I must confess I should much have liked to inspect the books of certain well-known and highly-respected native bankers of that city.

Time went on, when one day, many years afterwards, Sir Frank Souter received an official intimation from Nagpoor, requesting him to send up a European officer and good subordinates to take charge of a certain European "loafer" there apprehended, who declared that he was one of the 33rd regimental guard on duty on the night of the robbery, knew all about the crime, and where the treasure was still concealed. Sir Frank complied, and the loafer in question was taken safely down to Kalian, and thence up to Poonah. There he was supplied with a fatigue party, and they dug here, and they dug there, as he directed them. It is true, no doubt, that Poonah—the Wanowrie part of it especially—had immensely changed since 1858. Loafer alleged this change as his chief difficulty in "spotting" the place where the treasure had been buried. The men worked away indefatigably wherever he said. About 11 A.M., when the sun was getting mighty hot, and the fatigue party mighty thirsty, Loafer threw himself on the ground with roars of laughter, vociferating, "I've only been making hares of yer! I niver was in the 33rd, and I know just nothing. Years agone I saw an account in a newspaper of this 'ere robbery, and I thought I'd have a bit of a lark with it some day, and get down to Bombay."

By telegraph and by letter it was ascertained that this joker had never been in the Army at all; as a matter of fact, he was, in former years, a railway employé. He scored all round, for he could not be proceeded against. He got to Bombay, and was comfortably deported in due course to England.

No account of Bombay loafers would be complete without a reference to the harmless old fellow whose death, I think, I read of two or three years ago. For a quarter of a century or more, Collins, I believe he was named, was to be found somewhere or other squatted in some favourite nook in the Fort, his preference being for some lane opposite Watson's Grand Hotel. Many of us thought that he was an Armenian, and his features favoured this supposition. He never solicited alms—in fact, he never spoke, but there was a mute appeal in his sad, worn-looking eyes, a dignity in his grand face, with its long grey beard flowing to his waist, which attracted the passer-by, and made him forget the squalid appearance of this curious old fellow. Many a coin was silently passed into his hands by European and Native, and as silently received, to be immediately put away in some place of concealment in the bundle

COLLINS.

of indescribable rags which made up his clothes. He was popularly supposed to have lost his wits in his youth, after some great domestic affliction, but there was nothing in his eye that betokened a weak intellect—at any rate, he was quite harmless, and was officially tolerated by the Police. To what lair he retreated at night is best known to them. When he died, if I remember aright, a quite respectable sum of money was found about his person.

In conclusion of my brief account of loafers, and in support of my contention that Natives are wonderfully generous and kind to the mean white, it will be appropriate that I should recall a very touching incident that occurred during the visit of His Royal Highness the Prince of Wales to Bombay. The popular gaze was then towards royalty; the popular mind was almost entirely occupied with the great pageants that for a whole week followed each other in quick succession, so that this particular incident may not have been known to or noted by many persons.

Among the Political agents, each with his particular Rajah or Nawab in tow, who were summoned to Bombay for Lord Northbrook's and, afterwards, for the Royal visit, was Mr. C——, the gentleman who, I believe, was the first Municipal Commissioner of Bombay, the man who built the Markets called after his name. It was fully five years since his connection with the City had ceased, and certainly neither market-dealers nor stall-holders had the remotest expectation that he could ever do anything for them again. It was notorious, however, that they had on more than one occasion when he visited the market given him quite an ovation.

Now, it will be remembered that on a certain day, the 12th of November, 1875, it was arranged that as a part of the programme a "jolly good dinner" should be given to all the soldiers and sailors then in the City. The number of these who actually sat down ultimately was over two thousand.

While the preparations for this Gargantuan meal were progressing, a self-constituted Committee of the market-dealers asked the worthy Superintendent, Mr. Patrick Higgins, to co-operate with them, and to send Mr. C—— a sort of "round-robin," which was to the effect that they saw and heard on every side the extensive arrangements being made to banquet every one but the *poor* white man, such as the vagrants and the European convicts in the jails, the inmates of the Strangers' and other Homes, and the poor pensioners. To show, therefore, their gratitude to Mr. C—— in a way that he might accept, and that would be specially acceptable to him, they had determined on the same day, and at the same hour as the soldiers and sailors were to be feasted on the Esplanade, to give a good square meal to *all* the poor whites in Bombay. Details were left to Mr. C——, and they bound themselves to comply with any indents for meat, vegetables, bread, and groceries that Mr. Higgins, the Market Superintendent, should make. The American Ice Company gave ice *ad lib.*, and mineral waters in abundance were given by sundry other firms.

Not being on duty that day, I obtained permission to accompany the Rev. J——n R——n (who, I think, was out as a special correspondent for some newspaper) and Mr. C—— to all the places I have named above, where over one hundred and twenty unfortunate "mean whites" partook of at least as good a dinner as was given to Tommy Atkins and Jack Tar on the Esplanade. At each place a few words were said to the men, many of whom were visibly affected.

Yet it is commonly asserted that our Aryan brethren are destitute of the virtue of gratitude.

CHAPTER XXIV.

RECEIVERS OF STOLEN GOODS AND COINERS.

Receivers.

I HAVE as yet said little or nothing about receivers of stolen goods, or "fences," as they were called in former days—and still are occasionally—in London. I doubt if the King of the Fences—Fagin the unforgettable—combining the receipt of any and everything purloined with the careful culture of youthful criminals, is, or ever has been, known in the flesh in the far East. I do not remember that General Charles Hervey in either of his publications mentions one. I myself never encountered one. The education of thieves, pickpockets, burglars, and dacoits is almost a caste matter—a mere question of heredity. Thief, burglar, or dacoit follows the calling of his forefathers, stimulated by unwritten traditions, excited to emulation of the deeds of their elders around them. There is no place for a general practitioner like the accursed Jew.

Take away the educational side of this double-dyed scoundrel, and there remains but the mere common-place *rôle* of the receiver, and of these in

India, perhaps more than in any land, there has always been an *embarras de richesse*. Among the petty traders, Wanias, Goozars, Marwarris, and the like, it will scarcely be libellous to say that ninety-five per cent. have at some time or other in their lives been guilty of receiving stolen property, whether by way of purchase or pawn deposits, knowing, or having the best of reasons for supposing, it had been stolen. Even among the very well-to-do of these castes, and among the Brahmin and all Hindoo sowkars or bankers, there are not many who have not yielded to temptation when it has assailed them on a sufficiently large scale.

The nearest approach to Fagin, and by far the most dangerous to the public good, are those petty traders found in or near a cantonment where British troops are quartered. Even Rudyard Kipling will admit that there *are* some Tommy Atkinses in every regiment who are hopelessly bad, who were well known to the Police in England before they took the Queen's shilling, and that there are certain corps, very gallant in action, which contain, probably by reason of their recruiting-grounds being in tainted towns, a very large admixture of the semi-criminal classes.

Men of this stamp are not many weeks or days at their new quarters before they make acquaintance of Saloo Meeya, the rag and bottle and old iron collector; of Virchund, the obliging and obsequious Marwarri usurer; of Chimmapa, the tailor, and especially of Pedro, the half-caste Portuguese, where "best Europe" goods to eat and withal to drink are always obtainable on the easiest terms. A sort of freemasonry is speedily established between these worthies, and they stick to each other through thick and thin. Very soon an officer loses his watch, and if we were to follow Private Peterson into the Bazaar next morning, we should see him loiter about till he gives, unperceived, some signal at a certain shop, strolling off, whistling, to sneak round to the back for a brief interview with Saloo, or Virchund, or Pedro. Private Peterson would then come out wiping his moustache, and would be somewhat flush of cash for a time, while the Major's watch would be well on its way to Bombay or Poona, or elsewhere, in charge of some safe hand, long before anything in the shape of search was instituted. Suspicion would fall on the wretched "boy" or body-servant of the Major, probably just picked up in the Bazaar. He would be "led a life" for a time, perhaps be turned out of camp in the end, while the Mess would inveigh against the dishonesty of native servants.*

Stolen gems and pistols, jewellery and clothing, are just as easily disposed of through the same agency. Rupees in cash Peterson and Company promptly pouch, but bank or currency notes only find a market with the Marwarri and his class.

I had been but a few months in the country when

---

* *Nota Bene.*—To Congress-Wallas and their puppet M.P.'s. To all globe-trotters and all belittlers of their countrymen abroad! English officers do *not* habitually call their servants "*niggers*"—*damned* or otherwise—in India!

I was sadly victimised in the matter of notes. I had just been down from Satara to Bombay to pass my first examination, and, having come off with flying colours, easily obtained a month's leave, which I proposed to pass in Poona with dear old "Paddy" Hunt of the 78th Highlanders, a friend of my family. Before leaving Bombay I drew out 600 rupees from my agents, being the balance still to my credit of a liberal donation with which my father had started me in India. It was my intention to pick up a second nag cheap if I could, while sojourning with the 78th. I was advised to take up six Bank of England notes for £10 each, as being safest to carry, and likely to realise a good exchange up country. I stowed the precious documents in a brand-new despatch box, appending the key to my watch-chain. The second day after my arrival at Paddy Hunt's I opened the despatch box to get out a note, when, to my horror, I discovered that only one note remained out of the ten. The thief had had the grace to leave me one!

Hunt, as may be imagined, was very sore about the matter. *He* suspected my native servant, who was a man of the highest character, and had been all his life before in the service of a relation who had just retired, and left him to me. *I* suspected Hunt's soldier-servant, a particularly plausible Irishman of the name of Callaghan (the 78th Highlanders was half Irish in those days). It became so unpleasant, and moreover I had only just enough left to pay my way to Satara, that I cancelled my leave, and shook the dust of the little house at Ghorpooric off my feet.

About three months afterwards, I heard from Paddy Hunt that, in consequence of some angry words between two women in the Regiment, inquiry had again been taken up about my missing Bank notes. It appeared that the immaculate Callaghan was "carrying on" with a young woman in the Regiment. She met a braw Scotch woman, wife of a corporal, near the Canteen. The twain had been having "sups," and got to quarrelling, when the Scotchwoman taunted Callaghan's light-o'-love about Callaghan, adding, "that the vera claes she wore were bought from that puir English laddie's notes." Orderly Room was succeeded by Court of Inquiry, and although legal evidence was not forthcoming, no reasonable doubt remained that Callaghan had opened my despatch box by the very simple process (which I forgot to mention before) of driving out the pin that ran down the hinge at the back, and that he had disposed of the notes to a certain Marwarri shopkeeper in the neighbouring Military Bazaar.

The notes, however, were never traced. Why Callaghan should have left me one of them, except out of pity for the "puir English laddie," I cannot conceive. Anyhow, I was very grateful to him for his forbearance. It was believed that Callaghan himself only got fifty rupees out of the Marwarri! In the result, Callaghan went back to duty in the ranks, with a black mark against his name, and the Marwarri was turned out of the cantonments.

Most regiments in India, I believe, maintain a kind of Detective Police of their own in their Bazaar, and they are tolerably efficient in preventing drunken broils, but there should be a Civil Detective agency also working secretly with the Adjutant. A Commanding Officer cannot be too particular as to whom he allows to settle down in his Regimental Bazaar, for it is a loadstone which attracts all the most dangerous and dishonest characters in the country-side—at least one-half of the crime committed by or attributed to Tommy Atkins is instigated by these rascals. Then, again, it is a trite saying that if there were no receivers there would be no thieves.

COINERS.

Coiners in India, though professionals, are of any caste; more commonly they are of the "Sonar," or Goldsmith caste. They range throughout India more or less. In the Western Presidency they have never abounded, by reason probably of the great caution evinced by the masses of the people in taking over money for payment. Most of my readers must have noticed that, be the poor man who he may, year gardener, your coolie (labourer), hired by the day or hour, he carefully rings each coin on a stone before he finally ties it up in the corner of his garment. I have often seen the beaters out shooting thus test the four-anna bits I gave them. It is an irritating detail to any one, but specially to an official who

s

knows that he can have no cash that has not come direct from the Government Treasury. But, after all, it is only natural, and the reasonable inference is, that there must be much more base coin in circulation than is generally supposed.

At page 130 of the second volume of General Hervey's admirable book entitled 'Some Records of Crime,' he gives a graphic account of the process adopted in making false coin, which I shall take the liberty to transcribe, omitting certain technical expressions, which would be unintelligible to the English reader.

"The moulds used are formed from unslaked lime, and a kind of yellow clay, finely powdered and sifted. This, when moistened and well worked into a kind of putty, is pressed round about the piece of money to be imitated; the mould, thus rudely formed, is then pared all round of superfluous stuff, and is placed within some charcoal embers till it gets baked. It is then taken out, and when cooled enough its rim is carefully incised all round and the enclosed coin released, leaving an exact impression of both faces of it within the hardened amalgam. The two parts are next joined together with an adhesive stuff, and molten tin poured into the hollow interior of the mould just formed through a small aperture deftly drilled through the rim, which, when sufficiently cooled, is taken out, when lo! the thing is done, the false money ready to hand, it only remaining to smooth away the metal protruding through the drilled hole, and to rub the piece over with dirt or other colouring substance whereby to give it the appearance *of being old enough money.*"

I have found, or had found by my subordinates, plenty of these cracked moulds; for a new mould is required for every base coin made. General Hervey was writing from his diary of 1867, and he mentions the difficulty in coining the old Company's rupee "by reason of the rim being milled or grained." Coiners have made great advances in the twenty-five years that have since elapsed, and base coin is now turned out milled in the rim, quite "according to Cocker." The main difficulty now experienced by the profession is to get the weight right enough to pass muster in a crowd, and even then the provoking thing will not ring true. Still, a great deal of base coin *does* undoubtedly pass at fairs, pilgrimages, and other busy assemblages of ignorant natives.

Excellent imitations also are being made of the currency notes, especially those of the smaller denominations. Not a year elapses that the excellent Bombay City Police do not run in some gang of coiners or note-forgers. If this is done in the green tree, what will be done in the dry? When our enterprising friends learn some of the now many (say forty) processes by photo-zincography, and the like, for the exact reproduction of anything printed or photographed, what a harvest they will make for a while! The only wonder to me is that skilful note-forgers in England have not already been in the field, and that India has not been flooded with spurious currency notes of all values, prepared in Paris, and consigned to agents all over India for distribution. I shall be greatly surprised if at least one good haul is not soon made in this way.

CHAPTER XXV.

MISCELLANEOUS.

THE FIGHTING QUALITIES OF THE POLICE.

CONSIDERING the low pay of Policemen in India—the opportunities for massing them in any numbers for Military Education—that only about one-half of them are fully armed, and two-thirds of them only half drilled, it must be admitted that, since their reorganisation in 1853, the Police of the Western Presidency (and doubtless of the whole of India) have shown themselves fairly staunch under fire. When led by European Officers they often display a good deal of what the French term *elan*; when led by native officers only they are apt to develop that quality which is best described as "caution"—there is a manifest disposition to get under cover if any is available. But the same may be said of Jack Sepoy, who is recruited from precisely the same classes—systematically and thoroughly drilled—and perfectly acquainted with the use of the weapon he carries.

I have seen some very gallant rushes by a handful of half-armed, half-drilled, native Policemen—I have seen them hold their ground with the utmost determination against greatly superior numbers. Poor Sir Frank Souter, if he were alive, Captain Daniell, the Kennedys, and your worthy City Commissioner, Mr. Vincent, will certainly bear me out in this.

On some future occasion I hope to record events in which the Police of the Western Presidency greatly distinguished themselves. After all, they *are* worth looking after, for they make up, if I mistake not, at least fifteen thousand men in your Presidency, exclusive of Sind and your City.

Multifarious Duties.

The Policeman probably ranks second after that official Camel the "Tehsildar," or Mamladar (Chief Officer of a sub-district), in the multifarious nature of the duties he is called upon to perform. The latter, aided by the Chief Constables, have to give the orders, supervise their execution, and is responsible for the money part of the business: the Policeman has to carry them out. It is he who has to assemble the people if they are wanted in any particular numbers, as they often are; it is he who has to collect carts, camels, bullocks, forage—anything, in short, that the "Sirkar" may require, and he does it fairly well if he knows his range and the Patels, or headmen, in it.

I have seen them suddenly called upon to carry out the most extraordinary "fads" of the Government, or the Commissioner for the time being. For example :—

COLLECTING THE SPANISH-FLY.

Early in my career there was a certain very amiable Commissioner whose great idea was the development of the resources of the country, and in many little ways he did much good, which still bears fruit. It dawned upon him one day that a certain very offensive insect, which we all know as the "Blister-fly," had all the valuable properties of the Spanish-fly, or was really the same species, and that our Hospitals could be abundantly and cheaply supplied with Cantharides from our local stock of plagues. He accordingly persuaded the Government to grant a reward of so many annas per tola weight for the unsuspecting Blister-fly.

Out came the order, and forthwith all the available Police in the country were out with men searching for and collecting the noxious insect. I am afraid to say what this little experiment cost the State, or how many hundredweights of disgusting stuff was collected in various parts of the country, but I know the quest had to be stopped suddenly, at the instance of the terrified Secretary of the Financial Department.

It is fair, however, to mention that Cantharides have since been obtained locally for the Hospital Stores, so that perhaps in another quarter of a century the saving on the English price may wipe out the crushing first cost.

Snakes.

Shortly after the above incident, I was working in the same District with a Superintendent of Police, who went more or less mad about an antidote to a snake-bite. It was in the Southern Konkan, which is infested with these reptiles, and where the mortality from snake-bites each year far exceeds that of the whole of India.

Mr. C. claimed to have discovered that the administration of ammonia to the bitten man, with certain other simple remedies, such as lancing the wound, etc., was an almost certain cure. As a matter of fact, the use of *Eau de luce* and other forms of ammonia in snake-bite cases had been known for many years, but this does not detract from the merit of Mr. C.'s action.

With the dogged obstinacy of a Scotchman, he hammered away at the subject with the District Magistrate, Commissioner, and Government, expending his own money in distributing *Liquor Ammonia* in neighbourhoods where he could personally watch results.

His efforts were at last crowned with success, and sanction obtained for the issue of unlimited supplies of the needful drug. Government were "pleased to direct" that Mr. C.'s system and code of instructions should be extended to all Districts.

This involved the drilling of all the Patels, or head men—the distribution to them by the Police of supplies of Liquor Ammonia—the reporting of cases in which it had been used successfully, or otherwise. I believe in certain districts it is still *de rigueur* that every sub-district Office and every Police Post shall have a stock on hand. I have no doubt that in the past thirty years its use must have saved many lives, when the patient was in fair general health, and within reasonable distance of a depôt. I have

COBRA ON STRIKE.

myself often used it with success in cases of men bitten by the "Foorsa,"* the commonest of the poisonous snakes, even though two or three days had already elapsed; but I do not believe that in the case of the *Cobra*, or that hideous beast the Chain Viper,† it would have the least effect, even if it were exhibited within a minute of the bite.

* A small brown snake whose name I have not ascertained.
† Curiously enough called also *Daboia elegans*.

From trying to cure snake-bites to exterminating the reptile altogether was a natural step, and accordingly a few months saw the war of destruction begun, and again the Police were spread broadcast over the country to enlist the people's aid. It was very soon found that the rewards tariff had been pitched too high, and, if I remember rightly, it was

DABOIA ELEGANS, OR CHAIN VIPER.

cut down to an eighth of the original offer. Nevertheless, such myriads of snakes were brought in that the Government was compelled to cry, "hold—enough," and to put a stop to the war summarily.

I know that in the Ratnagiri District alone the expenditure ran up to over a lakh of rupees. Most of the snakes brought in were "Foorsas." The fact is, that one might as well undertake to weed the

Southern Konkan during the Monsoon as to extirpate the Foorsas in that country—they are to be found under every stone on every hillside. There are certain sub-districts in which there live thousands of poor Mhars who, always at starvation point, *do really* starve between July and September, which is just the time of the year when Foorsas are most easily found. It would be humane policy to give special grants for rewards for Foorsas brought in during those months in those particular sub-districts.

As to the deadly Cobra and the Chain Viper, the tariff should be much higher, for these really might, to a great extent, be extirpated in a few years.

You want to encourage the Mhars to hunt for them steadily and persistently, not to pay any one who happens to light upon a venomous beast and kills it. Remember, too, that these two terrible reptiles are apt to haunt the vicinity of dwelling-houses and the pastures. Many a goat or bullock dies mysteriously which has simply been bitten by the Chain Viper. I should greatly rejoice if I heard that the rewards for these species had been raised to $2\frac{1}{2}$ rupees each, or more.

The Great Famine.

It is unnecessary to dwell at any length on the exceptional services rendered by the Police during the Deccan Famine of 1876–78. Are they not still fresh in the memory of all those who worked throughout that awful calamity?

It was not merely that crime—especially offences against property—multiplied exceedingly, that each man had to do ten men's work, that he had to do it amid a starving population, among which he himself could barely purchase food, and in a country desolate exceedingly, many villages deserted, others with only a few emaciated wretches remaining in them.

Besides the abnormal increase of crime, which filled every jail and lock-up, and demanded extra guards, the Police had to aid the District Authorities to establish Relief Camps, to hunt up the starving, anywhere and everywhere, and to convey them to the Camp or the Relief Work. They had, moreover, to help in getting food grains from the railway stations into the interior, and they did it all without a murmur, and, I fear, with little or no reward.

The Locust Plague.

The Great Famine had passed away, the wretched survivors of the calamity had sown all the land they could, and were congratulating each other on the prospect of a decent crop, just then appearing above ground, when myriads of small hopping, caterpillar-looking grubs, very active in their movements, were observed marching on and over everything, and devouring every green blade that showed itself above the ground. There had been a few flights of locusts observed in the preceding year, but they passed unnoticed in the greater trouble of the Famine: they must have deposited their eggs over the country side—these were their grubs, soon to develop wings, and perhaps to breed again when arrived at maturity.

The Government rose well to the occasion, and spared no expense in attempting to destroy the insects as they marched. Again the Police were out all over the land, organising bands of beaters—instructing the heart-broken villagers how to use a hundred and one devices for the destruction of the foe. Trenches were dug, and lines of beaters drove the insects into them and buried them. Long, low calico screens, covered with gum or glue, were

THE LOCUST.

dragged along in lines, or were erected, and the insects driven to them, so that they hopped on to the sticky surface and stuck there. Lines of fire were ignited across the path of the enemy, and they were driven to them. The Government even imported an expert in the extirpation of locusts, which are the scourge of Cyprus, but this amiable gentleman could tell us very little we did not know well before.

Meantime, the insects waxed larger and larger, developed their wings, and in a week or so after doing so—presto! they took flight and went for the forests along the Western Ghauts, and thence, in vast, dense crowds, went out to sea, and disappeared into space, having devastated the crops over an immense area which had most suffered in the Famine.

It may be that in Cyprus, where the locust is ever present; it may be that in some of the American States which are annually ravaged by great swarms, breeding presumably on the slopes of the Rocky Mountains, some return may one day be realised for the vast expenditure incurred in dealing with this pest; but I am very sure that it is throwing away money to attempt to cope with them in India. They are ever present, it is true, in some part of the great Continent, but they usually stick to the forest ranges. If any casual visitors wing their way across the Indian Ocean, they too ordinarily settle first on the forests along the Syhadri range, and, according to my observation, take flight again, usually against the wind, over the ocean.

In one and the same hot season I saw clouds of locusts loading the forests on the south side of the slopes of Simla, and I encountered them in the "forests primeval" of North Kanara. It is not pleasant when you are just "posted" in your place up a tree in a beat for tiger to find the sun overcast by a cloud of full-grown locusts. As they come near you will observe vast numbers of crows and kites, and other birds of prey, skirmishing on the outside of the flying phalanx, and taking ever and anon a dive into the rustling mass. Once they are on you, you may give up shooting that jungle! They fly into your face—great ugly beasts three inches long—with a force that hurts considerably.

They mount on each other in myriads on the branches of large forest trees, till huge limbs are broken off by their weight, and a horrible fœtid odour accompanies them. Game, especially all the deer species, abandon the area they occupy, unable, probably, to bear the smell, or to browse on the herbage tainted by their droppings and the countless millions of dead that strew the ground. In ten days or so, however, after they have moved, the termites have done their scavenger's work, and the corpses are dismembered and carried off or eaten—a welcome storm comes down, and that nice young grass Bison and Sambhar love so well comes up with renewed luxuriance.

The lower castes of natives eat them in various preparations. They pickle them in salt, first plucking off the formidable serrated legs; they dry them in the sun and salt them—they press them into a loathsome-looking cake, which looks for all the world like mashed shrimps. They also have certain recipes for boiling, broiling, and roasting them. They say they are very good. I cannot say I ever had the courage to try any of these delicacies myself.

The Rat Plague.

As if famine and a plague of locusts were not sufficient to break down the wretched people, the year following (I think) an unkind Providence decreed a rat plague! The phenomenon has never been fully described; but I have not space in this paper to deal with it adequately. People do not believe it in this country.

Suddenly there appeared over all the districts that had suffered more or less from the Famine millions of rats, all marching from the east towards the sea. They were almost all of the very pretty species known as the Jerboa rat, shaped just like the mammalian of that name, and travelling in the same way by prodigious leaps. They too ate up everything as they went, gnawing off even the barks of trees. They burrowed and bred as they went along, travelling ever westward, chiefly by night. The Tanga ponies slipped on them as they galloped along with the mail-cart—they found out every store of grain, and destroyed the growing crops.

Then came the old story. All hands—including, of course, the Police—to the rescue! All Assistant Collectors ordered out to Camp. Large rewards were offered by Government, to begin with, for the trouble was that the people had got it into their stupid heads that these rats were, in fact, the transmogrified bodies of those who had died in the Famine!

It was some little time before this notion could be expelled, and the villagers induced to collect together and hunt the vermin. In the meantime, however, certain of the low castes, who have no particular prejudice of this nature, found rat-killing a very profitable employment, notably the "Waddars," or earth-workers, whom I have elsewhere described as the railway navvies of Western and South-western India, turned to with a will. They always eat these little rodents, and esteem them a great delicacy! And "what for no?" They—the Jerboa rats—are very delicate and dainty feeders, living entirely on grain, vegetables, and tender shoots. They are as fat as butter, and, when skinned, resemble a fat young rabbit, and, I am told, taste like one, too. There is a legend that an officer in charge of one of the Famine Camp Hospitals (then still crowded with patients suffering from the awful famine ulcer) needed flesh and meat for his patients, and hit upon the idea—

GERBILLE INDICA, OR JERBOA RAT.

and a very good one, too, *I* thought, in common with other officials—of giving them savoury stews of the little Jerboa. His patients visibly improved under the diet, but, alas! the Government got wind of it, and, fearful of the Native Press, peremptorily stopped the experiment by a Government Resolution, which made the over-zealous officer shake in his shoes.

Well, to make a long story short, the Waddars and the Mhars, the Khaikaris and all the outcasts, got to work. From a rupee a hundred, the reward speedily dropped to a few annas. The system established was this. All centres, such as sub-district offices, and all large or centrally situated villages in the affected area, were made payment depôts. The rat-killers brought their bags of dead rats to these depôts, where the tails of the corpses were cut off; the bodies were either taken away or burned, but the tails were tied up as vouchers into neat little bundles like radishes—until a supervising officer came round and checked off the vouchers against the amount disbursed. The supervisors (usually Assistant Collectors, or Police Superintendents, or Survey Officers) had to keep diaries, in which they would enter something like this—"*Visited Rampur; all right—counted ten thousand tails—burnt them!*"

I know that in two districts alone in the Carnatic, eleven millions of tails were thus accounted for! There were rumours, of course, of peculation, but a searching inquiry elicited no proof that there had been any. What amount of treasure this cost the State is a secret; it must have been immense, and it was just as much thrown away as in the case of the locusts, for what were ten or twenty millions of tails to the legions marching westward?

Finally, some tremendous falls of rain occurred, which drowned the vermin; the stream of pilgrims from the east dried up, and the rat plague was over.

Many theories regarding this phenomenon were advanced at the time, but I never heard but one that was at all intelligible. Prior to the famine—for generations past, in fact—when crops were abundant

T

and markets distant—it was the custom of the villagers to excavate "pews," or underground grain pits, lined with cow-dung, plaster, and straw, wherein to store their surplus grain, covering them with timber and a thick layer of earth. What the people would have done but for these hoards when the Famine broke out, God only knows! They were, of course, full of rats, but as granary after granary was cleared, the rats had to go elsewhere, and instinct taught them to travel westward, because to the east all was desolation: in the forests, in the country below the Syhadri range, there might be food of some kind—so the migration began, swelling to enormous numbers, as the little animals, with the marvellous fecundity of their species, bred and bred along the route.

I have dwelt thus, I fear, rather with too much prolixity for my readers on some—*only some*—of the multifarious duties demanded of the Indian Police. *Mea culpa!* I crave pardon! My object has been to show that the Indian Police have never shirked their work—that they have performed it invariably with zeal—that they have deserved well of the Government whose salt they eat. When Congress-Wallas, egged on by the "praying Mantis" order of of politicians, shall have introduced Anarchistical doctrines into India: when Asquiths shall there abound, I do not doubt that the Native Policeman will still be found equal to any task demanded from him. He will control and good-temperedly deal with processions of the great unemployed—the educated M.A.'s and B.A.'s of the country ; and he will dig and find, or not, as the case may be, explosives secreted about the country. But he must be dealt with in common fairness and honesty first ; and in my next and concluding chapter, I shall, with all humility, suggest how that should be done.

CHAPTER XXVI.

CONCLUSION.

I TRUST that I may have been to some extent successful, in the twenty-five preceding chapters, in bringing into strong relief the better qualities of our Aryan brethren, while gleaning from the field of memory the incidents most remarkable or best illustrative of the "seamy side" of Indian life.

It was my purpose, also, to indicate the weak points in a highly-important detail of Indian Administration. I have endeavoured to show that the Police, who are numerically equal to—perhaps even exceed—the entire British Indian Army, lack, for the most part, the detective element.* I will add here that this deficiency cannot be supplied, and their general *morale* can never be improved, *till they are sufficiently paid*.

It is of little or no avail that competitive examinations are held in England for young gentlemen to join as Assistant Superintendents of Police. This is simply beginning reform at the wrong end. It

* I always exclude the City Police at the three Presidency Towns—Bombay, Calcutta, and Madras. The police of the two first-named cities take the first rank with those of any in Europe.

is the rank-and-file who need attention, not the young fellows who are going to command them. These last, till Lord Roberts put down his foot, were usually selected from promising young Indian Regimental Officers, who had shown a predilection for Police work. No one will cavil at Lord Roberts's decision; he is invariably right in any matter affecting the Indian Armies he so long and ably governed. Superior Police Officers can even now be selected on the spot, without resort to England, from the Survey and Forest Departments, which possess exceptional experience of the country, and knowledge of the languages and the people. *Their* ranks can continue to be recruited from England: thus, a constant stream of excellent Superintendents and Assistant Superintendents might be kept up. Men show their aptitude and inclination for this kind of duty comparatively early in their career, so that a Governor or Lieutenant-Governor would have but to select from his list of qualified candidates.

But to return to the rank-and-file. In England the Police Force is a *corps d'élite* in its way. The best men are sought for, whether as to physique, general intelligence, or previous antecedents. They are obtained without difficulty, and, when obtained, receive a much higher wage than they could command in the fields of labour—they have good prospects of promotion, ample opportunity for showing the stuff they are made of—a comfortable pension assured to them for their old age. The whole world cannot show a finer body of men, for example—take them all in all—than the Metropolitan Police, who are thus recruited.

In India the rule is just the other way. A visit to the Head-quarters parade-ground of any District will satisfy any one that physique is not secured. Of all sorts, sizes, and heights, the men present the appearance of a collection of shambling scarecrows. They are willing (as I have shown) and fairly honest, but fifty per cent. of them, or more, are illiterate. Their antecedents are not usually bad (it is true), and many of them strike out to the front, and earn their small pensions meritoriously. But oh! they are so miserably paid! Horse-keeper—gardener—cow-men—the very coolie, or labourer, who works by the day—turns up his nose at the pittance the blue-coat Policeman receives. He is respected, because he is a man clothed (literally) in authority, but it is certain that he uses this authority in many petty ways to eke out his slender means.

The inevitable question will be asked—"Why should these things be?" "Are there not District Magistrates and Commissioners to point out the need of reform, and to suggest a remedy?" The answer is, that these Officers, for many years past, have never ceased pressing the question of Police reform on reluctant Governments. The pigeon-holes of the Secretariats must be full of printed and unprinted matter on the subject. Secretaries to Government must have written reams, clerks must have compiled hundredweights of "précis," and Honourable Members of Honourable Boards must have racked their brains in writing lucid Minutes on Police Reform.* "Why, then, has nothing been done?" is the next question. This brings us at once into a consideration of what the Government of India is.

It has been described as a complex system of cog-wheels. So it is, and a very excellent system, too—for India.

It is the creation of a hundred and twenty-five years or more of a foreign nation working among an agglomerate of races, creeds, and castes. A wheel has been added here and there as occasion arose: some new development created, some reform initiated, as opportunity and means were available. Cog-wheels have been taken out from time to time and cast away as worn out: others have been re-cast and replaced, without need for stopping the machine as a whole. So it must always be: a system of fly-wheels at full speed would long ago have jammed or broken the entire fabric into a thousand fragments. The machine is worked with the utmost simplicity by the Chief Engine Drivers—Viceroys, Provincial and Lieutenant Governors. The modern

---

* Lest I should be accused of exaggeration, I may mention after counting each item that the papers alluded to in the footnote to page 282—ignoring all that had passed before—began on the 22nd November, 1888, and terminated on 3rd February, 1894, thus covering four years and five months. The papers laid on the Editor's table (see the *Mahratta* of 18th February) enumerate seventeen letters, two telegrams, and four resolutions. Heaven only knows how many memos. and cross-memos. must have passed besides!

fuel consists of Government Resolutions, Minutes, and the like—and very well they burn. The lubricating material has heretofore been keen sympathy with the peoples concerned, the most earnest desire for their good, and the advancement of the Great Empire which shameless English Politicians now decry or endeavour to belittle. The worst and most dangerous lubricants—happily as yet of modern and only partial introduction—have been "Baboo-grease" and "Faddist-oil"; the former is a corrosive of the most virulent type; the latter, at present, is of milder action, but still dangerous. It is being used just now with opium, and will be comparatively innocuous until it be strengthened by "Party spirit" of English distillation.

I cannot refrain from quoting at this point some of the weighty words used by Lord Lansdowne on the 23rd of last January, in a speech which is, from the first word to the last, the utterance of an acute and able Statesman on the present position of India.

"On every side new difficulties and problems are presenting themselves, nor are they diminished by the habit of applying to a country, which is Eastern to the marrow of its bones, standards of treatment which are essentially European and Western. We cannot conceive England governing India as if it were one huge Native State. Under a British ruler the thing is impossible. We cannot turn back. All that we can do when we see inordinately strong doses of Western nostrums poured down Indian throats, is to protest as strongly as we can, and to endeavour, if possible, to stay the tide. Another danger, again—and I am not sure that it is not the greatest of all—seems to me to lie in the tendency to transfer the power from the Government of India to the British Parliament." (The speaker was interrupted at this point for some time by enthusiastic cheering.)

* * * * *

"There is no Act of the executive, British or Indian, which can be removed beyond its control. The Viceroy and the Secretary of State have alike to reckon with it, and there is no escape from its authority. It does not, however, follow that, because these powers are inherent in Parliament, they should be perpetually exercised by it; and it is the modern tendency to exercise those powers continually, and at the instance of irresponsible persons, which in my belief constitutes a grave menace to the safety of the Empire." (Loud and continued applause.)

* * * * *

"In the House of Commons an erratic member, in a thin House, may carry over the heads of the Secretary of State and of the Government of India a resolution vitally affecting the welfare of this country as summarily and as light-heartedly as if the proceedings were those of the debating club of a college rather than the senate of a great Empire. In a couple of hours the work of years may be undone; and so it may come to pass that, while we are slowly and laboriously striving to obtain an equilibrium between income and expenditure, or endeavouring to improve the condition of our Indian service, some haphazard decision of our masters on the other side threatens our finance with bankruptcy, or capsizes our most carefully considered schemes for improving the efficiency of the public services."

These words, and other sentences as terse and valuable on other Indian topics, ought to be emblazoned in golden letters on the panels of the Cabinet Council Chamber.

The question of Police Reform, like a hundred questions of more or less importance, has been from time to time shelved, to make room for whatever at the moment seemed the more pressing matter of the day. Famines, and kindred calamities, have stood in its way. Irrigation Works; Famine Relief Railways and their Feeders; Education, the great cormorant—with its technical and other greedy progeny;—all these have come from time to time—most unrighteously—in the way of Police Reform, in truth, the greatest, the most important of them all.

But Governors and Lieutenant-Governors want to make their mark, not so much in India as in England, where their career, if they are ever to have any career, will be. They have a short term of office, and at least the first half of it is occupied in learning some smattering of the people they are governing. Pageants and tours take up a great deal of their time, and they are naturally wary of identifying themselves with reforms which will have only local bearing, and may not tell effectively in their gubernatorial career as a whole.

Thus has the question of Police Reform been systematically "shunted," though several Governments, including Bombay, are understood to be strenuously striving to set their houses in order.* It is a matter, moreover, which unquestionably

* Since these papers have been in the publishers' hands the Bombay Police Reform Scheme has been sanctioned and "placed on the Editor's table." It shows a vigorous attempt by Lord Harris to right a great wrong, but, alas, the monetary difficulty was against him. Half a loaf is ordinarily better than no bread, but, besides that, the pay of the Armed Police has been left untouched. A dangerous experiment is to be tried with unarmed police on comparatively high pay. I need not indicate to any Anglo-Indian who has worked outside the Secretariat what that is.

involves increased expenditure; and for many years past, with the rupee steadily falling in value, there has been little to spare: no Governor would have dared to propose a substantial advance for Police purposes. Sir Richard Temple—who has done more for Western India than can be accounted in millions sterling in the one matter of Forest organisation—would certainly have brought Police Reform to the front had he but stayed. But there are not many Indian Administrators possessed of Sir Richard's energy and experience.

No man who has calmly considered the events of the past few months—be he Anglo-Indian or not—can fail to perceive the signs of coming trouble. *These riots are abnormal*; the Police are failing to curb, or, what is of more importance, to prevent them. The time has surely come when Police Reform has forced itself into the first rank of the great needs of the Government.

I do not know how many of my readers may have been encamped in sultry weather on tour—not a cloud in the sky, not a breath of wind to stir the leaves of the trees above us—when the trusty peon outside has suddenly opened the tent purdah, or "Chick" screen, and announced, "Saheb! Dibbil átá" (There's a devil coming). You look out and see advancing over the still, arid plain a thing like a waterspout, thickening and increasing in volume as it comes. It is a spiral dust storm (how raised—God knows!), sweeping over the country. Anon, it will be seen to pass over, suck up and disperse in fiendish wantonness huge stacks of forage standing in the fields below you, or playfully to snatch off the thatched roofs of the village a few hundred yards off. Lucky if it does not take your encampment by the way! If it does, then, despite of tent-pegs driven newly in, and all your screens braced down, you experience a blast of wind, hot as from a furnace, and

"SAHEB! BURRA DIBBIL ÁTÁ."

find your floors, your table, your bed, half an inch deep in sand. It passes, and all is quiet again, *but it is the infallible precursor of a storm of wind and rain.*

These riots here and there all over India seem to me to resemble "the devils" we used to know and grumble at. They are the forerunners of trouble, perhaps of an outbreak, which will tax all energies. A Reformed Police, well commanded, having in its body picked detectives communicating with the Commandants, will go far to ward off the impending evil.

If in the few preceding chapters I may have done injustice to any person or to any class, it has been unwittingly. In all my—not uneventful—career in India it has been painfully impressed upon me that between us—Englishmen—and the various races we govern "there is an impassable gulf fixed." Our ways are not as their ways, our thoughts and habits not as theirs. Thirty-five years have only made me more conscious of how little I really know of the people among whom I have lived so long and liked so well. It has been in a spirit of keen sympathy with them that these sketches have been penned. Farewell!

T. C. ARTHUR.

www.ingramcontent.com/pod-product-compliance
Lightning Source LLC
Chambersburg PA
CBHW030308240426
43673CB00040B/1103